EPIC LOVE STORIES

EPIC LOVE STORIES

BULBUL SHARMA

HARPER FICTION

An Imprint of HarperCollins Publishers

First published in India by Harper Fiction 2026
An imprint of HarperCollins *Publishers*
HarperCollins *Publishers* India, Cyber City,
Building 10-A, Gurugram, Haryana – 122002, India
www.harpercollins.co.in

2 4 6 8 10 9 7 5 3 1

P-ISBN: 978-93-6569-552-6
E-ISBN: 978-93-6569-435-2

Typeset in 11/15.7 Adobe Caslon Pro
by HarperCollins *Publishers* India Pvt. Ltd

Printed and bound at
Replika Press Pvt. Ltd, India

FSC www.fsc.org MIX Paper | Supporting responsible forestry FSC™ C016779

This book is produced from independently certified FSC® paper to ensure responsible forest management.

HarperCollins *Publishers*, Macken House, 39/40 Mayor Street Upper,
Dublin 1, D01 C9W8, Ireland

For 'D'

CONTENTS

INTRODUCTION

'There is a light that shines beyond all things on earth, beyond us all, beyond the highest heavens. This is the light of love that shines within us all.'

—*Chandogya Upanishad*

The moon is perpetually moving behind the clouds, the flowers forever fragrant and the celestial koel calling out endlessly in melodious tones. Almost every love story in Indian mythology is redolent with these romantic symbols from nature. For centuries, poets and artists have celebrated love by using beautiful, familiar images from nature, and continue to do so even today. This was my inspiration for rewriting a few of India's age-old love stories.

The love stories I have chosen are from the Ramayana, the Mahabharata, the Padma Purana, the Shiva Purana and the Bhagavata Purana. Written many hundreds of years ago, these stories reflect the myriad, complex emotions that surround a pair, either celestial or mortal, in love. The stories are woven in different hues, using a variety of threads, showing pure, romantic love, divine love, playful and joyous love, unrequited love, jealous love, mysterious love and tragic, sorrowful love. Though the lovers in each story travel down a difficult path and pass through many ordeals, finally, they always meet in a happy embrace either in this life or the next. As we read, they walk into the sunset in many different worlds.

We see the adulterous yet supremely divine, passionate love between Radha and Krishna. They meet secretly in quiet bowers, hidden from everyone's gaze, and recall how they had loved each other in earlier lives. Radha is not afraid and ventures out bravely at night to meet her divine lover. The love between Ram and Sita is pure and platonic while they are banished for fourteen years in the forest. A sad and forlorn Sita, far away from her beloved, pines away while Ram's heart aches for her. They can only talk to each other through the clouds and birds, and are fated to meet misfortune in their lifetime.

Love in separation is also the theme in various other love stories from the epics. The gorgeous demoness Hidimbi and the great warrior Bheema love each other with an undying passion, though they know they will soon be parted forever. King Shantanu too, spends a lifetime waiting for Ganga, his celestial love, to reappear, while Damayanti roams the forest all alone, crying for her lost husband Nala.

In some stories, fate plays cruel tricks on the lovers and their paths are fraught with untold miseries, but true love always wins. Urvashi and Pururavas's love story seems like it will end in tragedy, since a mere mortal should never fall in love with an apsara, but magically, the story twists into a happy ending.

Unrequited love, filled with deep sadness and constant yearning is the theme of Bheema and Draupadi's love story that never really happened. There is not a single affectionate word that comes Bheema's way from his beloved Draupadi, yet he never stops loving her. Unfortunate and doomed by the fates, Mandodari never stops loving Ravana though he does not reciprocate her devotion. In their lifetime, she is the epitome of a devoted and dutiful wife. She loves him till her dying breath and wishes to be his wife again in her next life, despite being treated so cruelly by him in this one.

Draupadi's passionate, intense love for Arjuna is tinged with anger, bitterness and jealousy. She loves no other, yet her deep desire for revenge also taints her love for Arjuna. She longs for him day and night though she knows he has other loves too.

Jealous love, tainted by curses, can be seen in the tale about the three great goddesses Saraswati, Laxmi and Ganga. All is not well in heaven as accusations and curses fly, and soon each goddess must part from their beloved Lord Vishnu.

Tragic, ill-fated love that shakes the three worlds is seen in the story of Sati and Shiva. Deranged by his beloved Sati's death, the great lord goes berserk and begins his eternal dance of destruction. The lovers are united once more when Sati is reborn as Parvati, but here too they must wait for the right moment to be together.

Savitri and Satyavan's love story could have ended in tragedy but the clever maiden won over the god of death by proving to him her true, undying love for her husband.

Shakuntala and Dushyant's story is also a tragic one because they are cursed soon after they fall in love. Shakuntala is abandoned by her husband for years, but she forgives him once she learns the reason for his forgetfulness and all is well in the end when the lovers are finally united. An uncommon love story is seen in Krishna and Rukmini's tale, in which she is happily abducted by her beloved lord. In Samjna and the Sun God's love story, we see a mysterious yet loving duplicity.

All is fair in love and love, shall we say?

The poems that I have selected to introduce each story are from the 1977 book of *Sanskrit Love Poetry*, translated by W.S. Merwin and J. Moussaieff Masson, that I was fortunate to have found in a public library years ago.[1] You will find that even though the poets wrote these exquisite lines of divine and mortal love centuries ago, they could be speaking about lovers—happy, unhappy, jealous, lovesick or blissfully joyous—today, because love transcends time and is truly without bounds.

---

1 Sanskrit Love Poetry. Translated by W.S. Merwin and J. Moussaieff Masson, New York, Columbia University Press, 1977.

I

RADHA & KRISHNA

Love Over Lifetimes

‘When spring came,
tender-limbed Radha wandered
Like a flowering creeper
In the forest wilderness.
Seeking Krishna in his many haunts,
The Blue God increased her ordeal
Tormenting her with fevered thoughts.’

—Jayadeva, Gita Govinda

‘Oh Krishna, dost thou not know the torment of
Radha’s soul, separate from thee?
She is a perpetual prayer whose fulfilment art thou.’

—Jayadeva, Gita Govinda

Radha stood poised on the threshold of her house, her eyes glistening in the moonlight. A koel, hidden in the shadows of the forest beyond, called out loudly, its piercing, incessant cry shattering the peace of the night.

Why was the bird calling at midnight? Was this a bad omen? Radha hesitated on the steps. She held on to the wooden frame of the doorway to maintain her balance. Her eyes were filled with fear as she gazed at the path ahead. She looked down at the steps that led to the forest. She only had to take seven steps down the silvery, moonlit path to reach her beloved Krishna, who was waiting for her in the dark, green grove of fragrant trees. Radha knew that to reach him she had to go beyond the boundaries of decorum and respectability. This was a reckless step for a married woman like her but she did not care anymore. She wanted to be with Krishna with all her heart. He was her true love and what did the rest of the world matter? All she could see, all she could think about now was her beloved waiting for her in the forest.

Radha felt her heart race as she lifted a foot and placed it quietly on the first step. Krishna's beautiful eyes flashed before her and she trembled as waves of longing flooded her entire being. She knew that as soon as their eyes met that she would feel faint, but he would reach forward and take her in his arms. He would hold her face in his hands and gaze at her till she drowned in his lotus eyes. The forest would echo with his joyous laughter as he spoke tender words to her and playfully tugged at her choli. Krishna, her beloved Madhav, was a vast, deep ocean of love in which she wanted to stay immersed forever. The earth stood still when she was with him and night and day merged into one blissful, never-ending moment in time.

Radha took another step. This time her bangles made a gentle tinkling sound and she stopped, turning around nervously. Everyone in the house was asleep. Only she was awake and stealing out like a thief to meet her lover. *What if someone woke up and asked her where she was going? What if they asked her who she was going to meet at this time of the night?* She had no answers and though she was beyond caring now, her heart suddenly gave a nervous flutter. How could she ever tell anyone about her secret clandestine meetings with Krishna? The koel called out again, filling Radha's heart with fear. She hesitated to take another step.

Then she heard the faint sound of a flute playing in the distance. Radha lifted her head to listen to its tune. Above her, the sky was a sea of darkness with the moon hiding shyly behind the clouds. Only a few stars lit her path now. The sound of the flute became louder. It was calling her repeatedly. Over and over, it seemed to call out her name. 'Radha . . . Radha' sang the notes, rising and falling. Her beloved Krishna was calling her. The strains, melodious and sweet as honey, came closer and closer and soon her entire being was filled with love for her beloved. Radha took another step forward. This time her foot stepped firmly on the path. The moon came out from behind the clouds and the silvery path now seemed to ripple in front of her like a river, and she felt herself flowing along in its waves. She heard a footstep behind her, someone called out her name but she did not turn to look. She lifted the hem of her skirt and began to run forward. She knew the silvery path would carry her swiftly to her beloved and her heart began to sing with joy.

The grove of trees, bedecked with white flowers, seemed to glow in the darkness as Krishna stood at its centre like a tall beacon of light. His dark blue skin shone like a polished sapphire and his eyes sparkled with love. Radha was overwhelmed with the brilliant image of her lord, which blazed like the morning sun suddenly appearing at night, and she could not move. Then the entire universe began to swirl around her as he took her in his arms and kissed her passionately. He kissed her over and over again till Radha was lost in a whirl of the divine madness of ecstasy.

It was as if they were together again as they had been for thousands of years and the eternal dance of the universe had begun once more. A thousand sapphire-blue images of Krishna swirled with her, each one more loving than the other. They danced the endless, ecstatic dance of love and Radha was a celestial queen once again. After they had made love, Krishna combed her hair and plaited it. Then he plucked flowers from a jasmine shrub and wove them into her hair. When it began to rain, he playfully sprinkled water over her and then draped her saree around both of them, before holding her in a tight embrace. The moon watched this exquisite play of love for a while and then slipped behind the clouds to hide the lovers from prying eyes.

'What if someone sees us? What if someone tells my husband?' Radha asked, looking anxiously into the dark shadows of the forest.

'Know me, my beloved. I am you and you are me. When we are together, we merge into one being. We become one soul. Who can tell us apart? Is there such a mortal in your family?' he answered as he caressed her hair. 'You wear my yellow robes, my peacock feathers and I shall wear your saree. You will be Keshav and I will be Radha,' he said, laughing.

'You may laugh but I am afraid, Keshav. My family is cruel and the people of the village will have harsh words for me if they find out I go to meet you in the forest at night,' said Radha, her eyes filling with tears. She knew she had broken the rules to be with her beloved and that she would do so again and again, but she needed Krishna's loving words to soothe her.

'Fear not, my love. I am here to protect you. No harm will ever come to you when I am here. Always remember this,' said Krishna as he took her in his arms. All of Radha's fears vanished from her mind as Keshav's lips touched hers. The sky opened up and showered rose petals upon them and even the moon could not resist coming out from behind the clouds once again to gaze upon this magnificent vision of the divine lovers.

The moon remembered how many lives ago Radha and Krishna lived and loved in the celestial city of Goloka—a city beyond Vaikuntha—Vishnu's heavenly abode. Everything was perfect in this blissful state as they danced their eternal dance of love, watched by the gods. Radha was a goddess queen, the divine consort of Krishna. She knew she was the chosen one. She knew she was the only one.

Thousands of years went by and then one day the sky suddenly went dark as thunderclouds appeared. Radha gazed at the dark clouds and knew that her life of endless joy was going to change. For the first time she felt a strange, burning ache in her heart. 'Is this fear?' she wondered.

Then one day, Sudama, Krishna's childhood friend, suddenly became enraged by her and, after a bitter quarrel, cursed her with these cruel words: 'You, who are so proud and vain will fall from your exalted position and wander the earth as a common milkmaid. You shall no longer be my Krishna's queen.'

As soon as Radha heard these frightening words she ran to Krishna. 'Save me, my lord. How shall I bear this curse? I will not be able to live without you even for a moment. You are my breath; my soul. I shall surely die,' said Radha as she fell at Krishna's feet, sobbing. Krishna lifted her up gently. He wiped the tears from her face and made her sit by his side. He already knew what was going to happen in the future and he smiled as he said, 'Why are you afraid? I will always be with you. As you are, so am I; there is no difference between us. Listen, my fair beloved, it is predestined that I too shall descend to earth. We will love each other once again in the forest of Vraja.'

The moon, remembering the loving words Krishna had spoken to Radha in another life, smiled quietly in the sky. In this life, Radha loved Krishna even though she was married to another. She had forgotten who she had been once and only knew the intense love she had in her heart for Krishna. But there were times when flashes of her past life came to her and she remembered for a few moments that she was the chosen one, dancing the eternal dance of bliss with her beloved.

As Radha lay in Krishna's arms, the sky changed colour and streaks of crimson began to appear. 'Dawn is breaking. I must go home,' she said, though reluctant to move away from Krishna's embrace.

'Stay a few moments more. Remember how we once made love when you were a young maiden? You were like an unopened lotus bud and I was a bee, crazed with love for you. My desire for you was so great that I created a storm and turned Vraja into a valley of rain and thunder,' said Krishna as he placed his hands softly on Radha's eyes.

The sky began to tremble and the light changed as they flew back together to a stormy day, years ago. Radha was a young girl when Krishna was born to Nanda and Yashoda in Gokula. One day, Nanda took his baby son with him when he went out to graze the cows. Suddenly the winds began to blow furiously and a strange dark blue light fell upon them. The trees lashed in the fierce wind as lightning flashed across the sky. Blinded by the dust of the sudden storm, a distraught Nanda was trying to protect his baby son when he saw Radha hurrying past. 'Take Krishna home. I will bring in the cows. Go quickly, Radha. The storm is getting stronger,' he shouted as the trees swayed dangerously in the wind.

Radha picked up the baby and ran as fast as she could. The lightning followed her and then stopped to create a circle around her, blocking her path. Radha froze. *Why had she been trapped in this strange circle of light? What was happening?* She could not see anything at all in this brilliant, dazzling light. Then a strange silence fell and she saw Krishna's face illuminated in the blue-gold radiance beaming upon them. She knew now that he had created this storm to be with her because in a flash of a moment she had been transported back thousands of years to their glorious celestial life.

She was once more Radha the goddess—longing to be with her beloved Krishna. Overwhelmed with desire for her lord, she yearned to dance, to sway like a flower in the breeze, to lose herself in the ecstasy of divine love. They looked into each other's eyes and she heard his honeyed, soft voice. 'My beloved, remember how we loved and played in the heavenly gardens? We touched moonbeams and gathered silver dust from the stars. We bathed in the dew from the celestial sky. I am here to fulfill the promise I made to you in that life. I had said that we will always be together and I am here with you now. Know that you are dearer to me than life.' In that circle of heavenly light created by Krishna, Radha closed her eyes and recalled every precious moment of her earlier life.

In her life as a goddess, her joy knew no bounds as they kissed and embraced. He loosened the garment that covered her body and, overcome with shyness, she hid her face. Her long plait unraveled and her dark tresses fell heavily like a rain-filled, dark cloud. Her bangles broke, her saree lay crumpled on the grass and the kohl from her eyes smeared her cheeks as Krishna kissed her and embraced her over and over again. Radha, lost in rapture, felt thousands of years rush past as she drowned in Krishna's love once more. She knew this moment of ecstasy would last for ever and ever because time did not exist for them anymore. This was a magical realm created for them to be together, for them to dance the eternal 'raas leela'.

Then Radha opened her eyes. She was alone. Krishna, her lover, her blue god, had vanished. The baby lay peacefully in her arms, gazing up at her with twinkling eyes. Radha held him gently and began walking towards Krishna's home, tears of happiness streaming down her face. Yashoda was overjoyed to see baby Krishna in Radha's arms. 'Thank the gods in heaven he is safe,' she cried as she took him from Radha.

Radha smiled. 'Yes. Thank the gods in heaven,' she said as she turned away her tear-stained face. The storm had subsided and the air was clear now. From that day on Radha knew that she would meet her beloved Krishna every day and every night. They would dance the raas leela together as they had done in another life. He had made a promise to her:

'In the sphere of the rasa, you will sport with me . . . As I am, so you are . . . I constitute your life and you constitute my life . . .'

Dawn broke, creating pools of light in the forest. Radha quickly retied her saree and gathered the broken pieces of her bangles. Krishna was not with her now, yet her entire being was filled with him. His blue skin was hers now and his beautiful lotus eyes seemed to have become hers too. She carried the scent of his divine body. Radha walked home slowly, her limbs heavy with languor. Cowherds and gopis walked past but they did not dare to speak to her or ask her where she had been. Radha walked on, graceful and glowing with an exquisite beauty they had never seen before. She was surrounded by a shimmering blue light that startled them all. They stared at her in speechless wonder. They all whispered and wondered but they did not dare to go near her. Only Radha, deep in her heart, knew the truth. Krishna, her beloved of thousands of years, was the truth; her blue god was the eternal, divine truth that lived in the core of her being.

2

HIDIMBI & BHEEMA

Love And Admiration

'"Do not go, my love" I could say,
But that is inauspicious.
"All right, go" is a loveless thing to say,
"Stay with me" is imperious.
"Do as you wish" suggests cold indifference.
And if I say "I will die when you are gone"
You might or might not believe me.
Tell me, my love, what I ought to say,
When you go away.'

—Bhartrihari

The demoness watched the twilight softly creeping over the forest as she lay, coiled like a huge, glistening snake, under a tree. Her pointed, bat-like ears were attuned to the slightest movement on the ground and in the air. Tall as a tree and with a powerful, massive body, Hidimbi could change her form as she wished but this gigantic, ebony-skinned, half-woman and half-demoness figure, was her favourite form.

Hidimbi looked around restlessly, her blue-black eyes gleaming like polished agate, waiting for darkness to fall. She could feel a turbulence in the air and knew that something strange and wonderful was going to happen; her heart could feel that the stars were planning to send love her way—a joyous and tumultuous love. Hidimbi knew that eternal love was not going to be gifted to her in her present life but she knew that love would happen and it would be intense and passionate but brief. 'How will I know love when it touches my heart? I have never felt this emotion,' she wondered to herself.

She gazed up at the sky. 'The movement of the clouds is swift and variable and I know the wind is going to change its direction as soon as twilight falls. Is there a celestial thunderstorm about to sweep through the forest, bringing a stranger into my life? What is going to happen? What are the fates churning up to change my life? Let it come—whatever it is. I shall embrace it with all my heart,' she thought. She was not nervous or afraid and calmly watched the light fading around her as a languorous warmth spread over her body.

Hidimbi looked at the last rays of sunlight dancing on the leaves when she suddenly inhaled a trace of a strange fragrance in the wind. 'What is this gentle yet heady scent that is making my heart ache with longing?' she said softly to herself. She held her breath and it seemed to her that a tiny flicker of light was glowing like an ember in the depths of her heart.

Later—many, many years later—when she was alone and trying to cope with the deep, sad longing in her heart, she often thought about that precious moment and she wished she had known that a perfect love was about to blossom. How she longed to go back in time and experience that exquisite moment when she had set eyes on her lover for the first time.

That strange, fateful evening, unaware that her future love was not very far from her, Hidimbi reached out and touched the tree trunk restlessly, her giant fingers tracing the bark, shattering it into fragments. Her strength always grew tenfold as soon as the sun set over the horizon and the forest became a sea of dark shadows.

She turned and looked at her brother Hidimba, who was sitting next to her, growling and scratching his massive head. He was twice as big and a hundred times stronger than her. Hidimba was full of hatred for mankind and loathed every living creature that crossed his path. A most feared rakshasa, he had ruled over this forest for centuries. Usually, he lay sprawled in their dark cave dwelling, smelling like a heap of rotting flesh and Hidimbi had to find food for him. Most days she went out alone at dusk to hunt but today, for some reason, he wanted to come out with her to catch their prey.

'Sister, you are getting lazy and never get me something substantial to eat. I feel hungry all the time. Let me show you how to catch a really enormous prey; a prey fit for a great demon like me.' He had growled, his ugly face distorted with greed.

Hidimbi usually hunted deer, wild pig, bison, tiger and even elephants or sometimes she caught fish in the stream if they were really starving.

Just yesterday she had brought her brother a massive stag to eat but she did not want to remind him of that huge meal. Hidimba always flew into a rage if she reminded him of what he had just eaten. His foul temper and his greed knew no limits.

As the light began to fade, they both rose and started walking through the forest. The earth trembled under their giant feet, rocks crashed and all the wild animals ran away to hide as swiftly as they could. A cluster of dried leaves floated down from the trees on to her shoulders and a peacock scuttled away from the path as Hidimbi raised her head and sniffed the air.

Suddenly, she stopped. Her sharp nose had caught the powerful, alluring scent of humans. She could see that her brother had sensed it too. He was always greedy for human flesh and often ordered her to go out to find some humans for him to eat.

Now, as they waited, the wind changed direction, carrying the scent of the humans even closer towards to them. Hidimba gave a deafening shout of delight. He leapt up into the air and landed on a hill nearby. He began looking around furtively. 'Where are these wretched humans?' he shouted from the top of the hill, his hunger making him insane with rage. He jumped higher and landed on a tall tree.

Then, from his perch, he saw a few humans walking in the grassy fields but then they disappeared from his sight. 'Sister, go look for them. Bring them back quickly. I have been dreaming of eating some good human flesh for days,' he said, swinging from branch to branch, drooling in anticipation.

Hidimbi was not really keen on eating human flesh but she could not refuse her brother. He would go mad with rage if she did and thrash her. Hidimbi reluctantly turned to follow the scent. She walked with heavy feet, going deeper and deeper into the forest, but could not see any humans. All she could sense was the sweet fragrance that had touched her heart not so long ago.

After walking around for a few hours, she lay down to rest under a tree and soon fell asleep. She woke up after an hour, still floating listlessly in a strange dream she had just had. A handsome, powerfully built human was holding her hand and they were walking through the forest, while a shower of flower petals cascaded down upon them from the sky. 'What an odd dream! Why should I hold a human's hand? Am I going mad? I have never even looked closely at one except to snap his head off with my hands,' she thought.

'I better go now and look for these humans before Hidimba starts a rampage through the forest,' she said, yawning and stretching her huge arms over her head. She rose slowly, her dark eyes piercing through the gathering shadows, and then she gasped.

Her gigantic figure froze but she felt a strange exhilaration sweep over her as she saw Bheema for the first time. Taller and bigger than any man she had ever seen, he sat silently on a boulder, gazing into the forest, his skin shining like polished gold in the moonlight. 'Who is he? How has this most handsome human creature in the world, in the entire universe, come into our forest? O! I must stay calm. I must stay silent or he might flee. I cannot let him go away from my sight,' thought Hidimbi as she stared at Bheema, her heart racing wildly with excitement.

As she gazed at him, her gigantic body began to shake; it was as if lightning had struck the very core of her being. 'What is happening to me?' she cried, keeping her voice low. Hidimbi's enormous form began to tremble and a strange, uneasy feeling raced through her heart. She felt her knees becoming weak; a fine sprinkling of sweat covered her mottled, dark skin and she began to feel faint. 'Why am I feeling like this? I am the powerful Hidimbi. I am unmatched in battle with any rakshasa. Why should a mere human affect me like this?' she wondered as she stared at the human, unable to take her eyes off him. Then she began to moan, clutching her huge hands to her heart, which was fluttering like a trapped bird.

'Could this be love? Am I falling in love?' she whispered, letting the joyous feeling overwhelm her entire being. For the first time, Hidimbi realized to her amazement, her heart could feel this intense emotion called love; her heart could fill with desire for a mere human.

She sighed and the forest echoed her moans.

Bheema, always alert, heard a faint, peculiar moaning sound and looked up. Hidimbi felt his eyes on her and in a flash of a moment, she changed herself into a beautiful human woman. She was no longer the massive demoness with wolf-like fangs. She had taken the form of a tall, graceful woman with a lovely face and sparkling jewel-like eyes. Bheema gazed at her, wondering what this wondrous, beautiful woman was doing in this wilderness all alone.

'Who are you, gracious lady? Why are you all alone in this dense, lonely forest?' he asked.

Hidimbi stood silently, wringing her newly formed tiny hands, uncertain of what to say to this man. She, whose terrifying roar could be heard all over the forest, had suddenly forgotten how to speak; she who could devour any creature in a few minutes had forgotten how to look into a human's eyes. An unfamiliar feeling of shyness flooded over her as she stood with her head bowed. She did not know who she was any longer; she did not know how to behave with this human creature who had changed her entire being in just a few moments. She was helplessly in love with him though she had not known what love was till this very moment.

She looked at Bheema, her eyes brimming with love and nervousness at the same time.

'Should I tell him the truth? Should I tell him that I have come to kill him and take his body for my brother to devour?' she wondered, as confused thoughts raced through her head. Then she noticed a few other humans lying on the ground. They seemed to be asleep.

Bheema saw her glance towards the sleeping figures and said, 'I am Bheema. This is my mother Kunti and my four brothers. I am guarding them as they sleep. We have been walking through this forest for days and tonight they felt too tired to walk any further, so they fell asleep under this tree. Who are you?' he asked again.

Suddenly, like a torrent, words tumbled out of her mouth, sounding unfamiliar to her own ears.

'I am Hidimbi. My brother Hidimba is a demon who rules over this entire forest. He has sent me here to kill you all,' she said in a rush, unable to hide the truth from him. Bheema gave her a surprised look. He could not believe that this beautiful woman with gentle, doe-like eyes was a demoness. As he was wondering what to say to her, they heard a furious roar.

Hidimba had snuck up on them. He leapt down from a tree and stood before them, his mottled, ugly body stained with blood. His huge mouth was half open as he drooled, swaying his massive head from side to side.

'You wretched, sly creature,' he shouted at Hidimbi, baring his fangs. 'I sent you here to kill this human and now I find you are trying to entice him with womanly wiles. Let him see your true form, ugly sister of mine, and let him be frightened to death. Show him your real "rakhshasani" body. Do it right now. I order you, sister, or else I will kill you along with this human creature.'

As she watched her brother move towards Bheema, Hidimbi made up her mind at once. She knew she had to protect Bheema otherwise her brother would kill him with just one blow of his mighty paw. She moved forward clumsily, hampered by her human and fragile form when she suddenly saw Bheema turn towards her brother.

'Come fight me, you monster. Leave your sister alone. Don't you know who I am? I am the son of the wind god. I am Bheema,' he said, striding forward to face Hidimba boldly.

Hidimba laughed and turned around to look at Hidimbi. 'Look at this puny human, trying to threaten me. Since you have betrayed me, sister, I will kill you first and drink your blood. Then I will slowly eat this human who has captured your black, disloyal heart,' said Hidimba. But before he could touch Hidimbi, Bheema leapt in the air with a roar and landed on the rakshasa's shoulders.

They struggled and fought, and as they battled each other—the demon and the son of the wind god—the earth began to tremble. Creatures of the forest came out of their hiding places to watch this fierce fight between a man and a demon. An entire night and day passed and twilight crept upon the forest again but the battle went on.

Hidimbi wanted to help Bheema, but he pushed her away. 'Watch me destroy this demon,' he said in a jubilant voice.

'You have to kill him fast. The sun is almost setting over the horizon and his strength will become more powerful when night falls,' she said. She felt a brief moment of regret as she spoke these words; she knew she was betraying her brother but then his evil, cruel image loomed in front of her eyes and she did not care if he was killed in this battle. He had tormented her for so many years and now he had finally met his match.

The fight carried on and then finally, just when the sun was about to set, Bheema picked up Hidimba and threw him over the rocks, breaking every bone in his body. Exhausted, his body covered with wounds, Bheema stood glaring down at the rakshasa as Hidimba breathed his last.

Hidimbi came forward and stood by Bheema quietly. Tears welled up in her eyes as she gazed at her brother's inert body. She felt only a fleeting twinge of sadness that he had been killed. 'He was a cruel monster, hated by everyone. He will be born again as a better soul,' she thought.

'Come, let me take you away from this evil forest. Let me heal your wounds. Let us go where we can be alone together,' she whispered, touching Bheema's hand. In response, Bheema shook his weary head sadly. He had fallen in love with this demoness who looked like a human woman but he was not going to leave his mother and his brothers.

'I wish I could go away with you but how can I abandon my family? They will perish without me,' he said, gently caressing Hidimbi's face.

'I can grow to a mighty form and carry them all to safety,' said Hidimbi. She was not afraid of showing her true form to Bheema because she knew that he loved her as much as she loved him. So she quickly turned into her real towering self. Bheema gazed at her in admiration. Her massive form, her glowing dark skin and her huge flashing eyes made her more enchanting in his eyes. He could not believe how powerful and strong she was.

'You were meant for me, my love,' he whispered, holding her in his arms.

Then Bheema turned his head as he heard footsteps. He saw his mother Kunti and his brothers walking towards them. Hidimbi stepped away from Bheema, unsure of what would happen now. The Pandava brothers looked at Hidimbi with surprise and when Bheema asked Kunti for her blessings to wed Hidimbi, they smiled and embraced their brother. 'You have lost your heart to this forest maiden,' they said. Kunti gave her permission at once and Hidimbi and Bheema both bowed their heads, unable to hide their joy.

In a flash, Hidimbi assumed a huge bird-like form and carried them all to a serene meadow beside a lake. Using her magical skills, she built for them a large hut, surrounded by fruiting trees and flowers. After she wed Bheema in a simple forest ceremony, Hidimbi folded her hands and bowed before Kunti.

'May I have your permission to take your son away? I promise to bring him back every night so that he can guard his family,' she asked shyly.

Kunti smiled and agreed. She could see how much in love her giant of a son was with this strange, beautiful creature.

Hidimbi put her arms around Bheema and together they flew high into the sky. When they reached a secluded mountain valley, Hidimbi slowly descended. 'This will be our home, my love,' she said, pointing to a green bower surrounded by tall trees. They spent hours together in their lonely forest home in total bliss. Bheema wanted to see the entire land so she flew into the sky every morning, carrying him.

As she roamed with her husband all over the earth, Hidimbi's heart was filled with happiness, though she knew they did not have much time together. She had used her powers and caught a glimpse of the future. Bheema would be hers only for a year.

'We must make the most of our precious time together. I want to spend every waking moment with you,' said Bheema, because he too knew they could not be together forever. 'Let us forget about the future. We are together now. This golden time is ours.'

They roamed the forest eating wild fruits that Hidimbi plucked for Bheema. They drank water from the fresh springs that Hidimbi found for him. She looked after her husband's every need and he in turn cared for her with a rare gentleness, as if she were a fragile creature and not a powerful demoness.

They spent their days lying on the soft grass, telling each other stories. Bheema talked of his endless conquests on the battlefield and Hidimbi told him about the mysterious creatures she had seen in the forest. She told him about the lions, elephants and tigers she had caught and tamed. Bheema poured his heart out to her like he had never done to anyone else in his life. He told her how angry he was at his fate yet he was helpless to do anything. 'I cannot disobey my older brother though his gambling has ruined our life. We have lost our kingdom and have to live like paupers now. Still, I love and respect him and have a duty to protect my family,' he said, letting Hidimbi's rough hands wipe his tears away. He knew that this demoness who stood so tall and proud had a soft, tender heart.

The days passed peacefully and Hidimbi's love for Bheema grew more powerful each day. He sang to her and wove flowers in her hair. He caressed her with his rough hands and kissed her gently even when she was asleep. Hidimbi thought she would drown in this sea of love. She wanted to do something that they would never forget. 'Come. I will make you see the universe with my eyes so that you will always remember our life together, even though it is so brief,' said Hidimbi one day, as she reached out to Bheema and clasped his hand.

Together they flew, high into the sky, beyond the clouds. As she carried her husband over the sun and the moon, then over the stars, and then circled over high mountains and oceans, Hidimbi's heart was filled with happiness; it was filled with a pure joy she had never known before. Though she knew their love was going to be short-lived and Bheema would leave her one day, he was with her today; at this moment he belonged only to her. She held on to him tightly as they flew over the clouds and softly kissed his forehead.

As they explored the earth, Hidimbi looked down and spotted a vast, emerald green valley nestled below a circle of mountains. 'Let us spend a few days here,' she said, and began to descend. So they lived together in bliss in this valley amidst flowering trees and scented flowers. Every evening, Hidimbi would faithfully carry Bheema back to his family. The days were passing by fast, and she was happy yet sad because she knew not much time was left for them to be together. She counted every moment as a gift because every moment with Bheema was precious to her.

One day, Bheema turned to her with a sad look in his eyes and she knew at once what he was about to say. 'Our time together is nearing its end. I have duties to fulfil which will take me away from you forever.'

Hidimbi did not dare show her tear-stricken face to her beloved, so she bowed her head. 'I know, my love. I want to tell you that I am with child. I beg you to stay till our son is born,' she said.

Bheema gave a roar of delight as he held her in his arms. He kissed her over and over again. Their happiness knew no bounds and now their love for each other was even stronger than before. They both knew there was not much time left but they tried not to think about the future. 'Come lie close by my side. Let me love you so that we both remember our love for each other; so we never forget what we felt for each other,' said Bheema, embracing his demoness lover with all his strength.

A son was born to them after a few months and then one day, as Hidimbi watched silently, Bheema left her and walked away. He dared not look back at her since his heart was filled with such deep sorrow that he was afraid he might break his vows and return to her.

Hidimbi did not shed a single tear as she picked up her newborn son and held him tightly in her arms. 'You are the cherished fruit of our love, my son. You will be my life from now.' This child would grow up to be as brave and powerful as his mother Hidimbi and his father Bheema. He would be called Ghatotkacha—one of the greatest, most courageous warriors in the battle of Mahabharata that was to come.

3

SATI & SHIVA

A Love Devastated

'Arise, arise! O my beloved Sati!
I am Sankara, thy Lord;
Look, therefore upon me
Who has approached thee.
With thee, I am almighty
The framer of all things,
Giver of every bliss.
Without thee, my energy!
I am like a corpse,
Powerless and incapable of action
How then, my beloved
Canst thou forsake me?'

—Vaivarta Purana

The clouds floated slowly across the mountain peaks, and as their shadows fell on the valley below, a young girl ran along the mountainside, graceful as a deer. Sati liked to spend all her time in the mountains, gathering wild flowers, watching birds and wild animals in the meadows. Sati was blissfully happy to roam around, free as a dancing cloud, but her family frowned on this unladylike behavior. She was, after all, the daughter of Daksha—the great Prajapati—who was such an important man that even the gods treated him with immense respect. Daksha, extremely proud and conscious of his high status, did not consider it proper for Sati to behave in this wild, rustic manner. She was not a simple village maiden; she was a princess living in a glittering, golden mansion and, according to him, she was to behave with a certain decorum.

Sati was often reprimanded for roaming around alone in the high mountain valleys and meadows but she did not care. While her numerous sisters dressed in fine silks and jewels and sat around demurely in the palace chambers, Sati was happy to dress in simple attire and she never adorned herself with jewels. She loved flowers and her delicate beauty was enhanced by the scented garlands she always wore in her hair.

One day, Daksha, her imperious father, was in a foul mood. He was furious with his daughter. The reason for his anger was not Sati's carefree ways but her steadfast, everlasting love for Lord Shiva.

All the gods paid their respects to Daksha ever since he had become the Prajapati—all except one. Lord Shiva refused to bow to Daksha or even acknowledge his presence. Mahadeva was content to live a simple life on Mount Kailash, hidden in the high Himalayas. He did not care for status or position and laughed at all the pomp and show that Daksha surrounded himself with ever since he had been made the Prajapati. Daksha, his vanity hurt, could never forget being snubbed by Lord Shiva and now hated him with a passion. He called Shiva an outcast; he ridiculed Shiva's ragged appearance and his nomadic, wild ways.

Daksha was outraged when he learnt that his daughter Sati wanted to marry Shiva. 'I will never allow this match to happen!' he roared. What he did not know was that Sati had loved Shiva ever since she was a little girl. For years, she had prayed with his image in her mind and she wanted to marry nobody else but the great Lord Rudra, even though she knew her father was vehemently against this match. 'It is only Shiva for me or else I will remain unmarried,' she said quietly, not caring what her parents said.

Daksha, who was already livid with rage, went berserk when he heard this. 'How can a daughter of mine choose such a man? Shiva is not of sound mind; he lives like a naked ascetic. He calls himself a god but goes around dressed like a beggar. He wraps snakes around his ash-smeared body and his only companions are ghouls and monsters. He has no fixed abode, and they say he lives in a cave with wolves and tigers. I will never allow Sati to marry him,' he shouted. His wife and daughters trembled in fear, but Sati was not afraid of her father's wrath.

In private, Daksha's wife Prasuti quietly reminded him that even when Sati was a child she would recite Lord Shiva's name over and over again.

'How does that matter? He will never wed any daughter of mine. I will arrange a swayamvar for Sati and invite all the important gods. She will have to choose one of them,' he declared and ordered his wife to make arrangements for a magnificent swayamvar at once.

Sati was thrilled when she heard about the swayamvar. Now Shiva would come to the ceremony and she would put a garland around his neck. They would be wed. Her dream would come true at last. She smiled as she walked along a mountain stream, chanting Shiva's name. Her heart filled with joy and happiness as the name, so beloved to her, echoed all over the hillside.

Sati, innocent and trusting, did not know that her father had other plans.

Daksha, simmering in anger, thought about the day Lord Shiva had passed by, ignoring him when he was made Prajapati by Brahma. Everyone who had been present at the ceremony had praised him, lauded his great achievement and had bowed their heads with respect, but Lord Shiva had just walked past as if Daksha did not exist at all. The Prajapati, full of his own self-importance, could never forgive Shiva for this slight. The dark and bitter memory of that insult had never left him and it gnawed at his heart constantly. His hatred for Shiva was like a blazing fire.

On the day of the swayamvar, Sati, for once, dressed herself up in fine silken robes and jewels. She was going to marry Lord Shiva and she wanted to look like a beautiful, bedecked bride for her lord.

Sati walked into the hall, her beautiful eyes darting around for the great lord, her heart filled with hope, love and joy. In attendance were many handsome, brilliantly attired gods sparkling with jewels, seated in the glittering palace hall, but she could not find Shiva amongst them.

Her eyes filled with tears as Sati realized what her father had done. The great Prajapati, her own father, had cheated her. Lord Shiva had not been invited. She bowed her head and began to cry softly.

'Come. Hurry. Choose a husband for yourself. Do not keep these important lords waiting and dishonour me,' hissed Daksha in her ears.

Sati stood very still. She raised her face to the heavens and began to call out Shiva's name. Her heart, her entire body, was engulfed in just one name. 'Shiva. Shiva. Shiva,' she said under her breath, over and over again. Sati was floating in her own world now. She could not hear anyone or see anyone in the vast hall; Sati was now surrounded by a blue light as she continued to chant her beloved lord's name. Her voice rose higher and higher, touching the roof of the palatial hall, making the pillars tremble, and everyone present looked at the beautiful girl in awe.

Suddenly, with a thundering roar that made the entire world tremble, Shiva—the mighty god of eternity—appeared. A gentle smile played on his handsome, rugged face. He reached out and placed his hand on Sati's head. Waves of joy ran through her body as Sati lifted the garland and put it around Shiva's neck. The gods watched, their eyes blinded by this dazzling, celestial light and then, when they realized that Lord Shiva had appeared in their midst, they bowed their heads. All except Sati's father Daksha, who stood still, speechless with rage. But he could not do anything since his daughter had chosen Shiva in front of all the assembled gods. He watched quietly, simmering in anger.

'I have no chariot waiting for you, my beloved,' said Shiva with a gentle smile as Sati looked at him shyly. 'We will have to travel on my faithful Nandi.'

So, as the gods applauded and showered flowers on the couple, the clouds parted and they sped away to Shiva's abode, hidden in the snowcapped peaks of the high Himalayas.

Seasons passed; the hills changed colours. Sati was blissfully happy in her remote mountain home. She sat in the grassy meadows, weaving garlands of wild flowers, and gazed with love and wonder at her husband. Though he had no material riches or glittering palaces to offer her, she loved him with all her heart.

'I was born to lead this life. I was born to be with you,' she said to Shiva whenever he asked her if she minded their simple way of life.

One day, while they were sitting on a hill and watching the sky change colour, surrounded by snow leopards and bears, Sati saw several chariots fly past carrying gods and goddesses and various demi-gods too.

'I wonder where they are all going in such a hurry,' she said to herself.

Lord Shiva read her thoughts and answered.

'Your father is holding a great yagna. He has invited all the gods. See how they have adorned themselves with their best robes and jewels. Each one is trying to outdo the other. Such vain creatures; even peacocks in the forest behave more modestly,' said Shiva as he roared with laughter, his handsome face glowing with amusement.

Sati did not smile. She watched the chariots racing past and her heart was filled with sadness and anger.

'My father has invited all the gods except for you. You are the greatest one and you are not going to this yagna. How can my father do this? It must be a mistake,' said Sati with a worried frown.

'How does it matter? You know I do not feel happy going to yagnas or any large gatherings. I am happy in our quiet abode where nobody can disturb me. And with you by my side, I can ask for nothing more,' said Lord Shiva in a soft voice, looking at his wife with love gleaming in his dark eyes.

Sati turned to him and said, 'I wish to go to this yagna. I will go and ask my father why has he done this.'

'I do not think you should do that. We have not been invited. Why should you go?' said Shiva.

'Why should a daughter need an invitation to visit her father's house? All my sisters will be there with their husbands. I would like to meet them,' said Sati. 'I am sure my father's invitation has gone astray. How can he not invite us to this important yagna? Do allow me to go, my lord,' she implored, her voice tinged with anxiety; a frown on her beautiful face.

Shiva sighed and gave his permission reluctantly. He was not happy about Sati going to her father's house but he did not want to refuse her anything.

'Go if you must, but I am afraid for you. I will send some of my helpers with you,' he said.

Accompanied by various strange, ghoul-like spirits who were Shiva's helpers, Sati set out for her father's home. She was looking forward to meeting her mother and her sisters again. When she arrived at her father's opulent palace, she saw all her sisters dressed in their finery, accompanied by their equally fine-looking husbands; she saw all the gods and demi-gods sparkling in jewels and she noted that even the apsaras were dressed in their most dazzling robes. They looked at Sati, clad in her simple saree, and unadorned with any ornaments, and turned their faces away. Sati rushed to greet her father. She was stunned to see that he refused to greet her and looked at her as if she were a stranger. Even her sisters ignored her as if she were a nobody.

Sati, bewildered and unhappy, looked at the gods seated around the yagna fire. 'Why are all the gods here except my lord Shiva?' she said, distraught and angry. 'Father, tell me. How can a yagna take place without the greatest of the gods present?'

'Who are you calling the greatest of all gods? That wild husband of yours who clads himself in animal hides?' said her father in a sneering tone.

'Father, please do not speak about my Lord Shiva like this. He is the greatest of them all. Ask any god present here and they will tell you that I am speaking the truth. Mahadeva is the greatest of them all,' said Sati, trembling with rage and humiliation.

'Stop talking about your wretched beggar of a husband. I did not invite him here because he brings his filthy companions to auspicious ceremonies and pollutes them, and I will not allow it to happen at my yagna. Remember,

I am Daksha. I am the Prajapati. I know the correct form of behaviour. Go away and sit quietly. Do not mention your uncouth husband's name to me again,' shouted Daksha.

Sati's eyes filled with tears. She put her hands on her ears to block out her father's tirade. 'I will not hear a word against my lord. You will not speak like this about him. Nobody will dare say a word against him,' Sati said, facing her father like an angry tigress. 'Shiva is my lord. Shiva is the greatest god. I pray to his mighty presence. I will atone for the great wrong that has been done to my husband today. Shiva, my great lord. Hear my prayers,' she repeated over and over again and then her voice started to break. Her entire body began to sway and then, suddenly, she fell down on the floor.

As the assembled gods and goddesses watched in fear, Sati, the beloved wife of Shiva, gave up her life.

An eerie silence fell over the assembly and Daksha stood quietly, wringing his hands. He was suddenly afraid. No one knew what to do now. Sati's mother and sisters began to weep, surrounding Sati's body as it lay on the floor.

Then with a screeching, hissing sound, a flame rose out of nowhere and began to spread rapidly. The walls of Daksha's opulent palace began to crumble and its pillars collapsed one by one. Giant, ugly demons appeared and began to attack the assembled gods. Everyone ran around frantically, trying to flee these frightening creatures. Suddenly, the palace was crawling with strange, ferocious ghouls and they picked up whoever they could find and cut off their heads and tore apart their limbs. The sacred fire of the yagna swiftly turned itself into a deer and fled.

Lord Shiva, tall and majestic, his face distorted with dark, smouldering rage, stood in the middle of this pandemonium with Sati's lifeless body in his arms. With tears running down his face, he began to howl with pain and his voice echoed all over the three worlds. The earth trembled and began to crack as people tried to escape Shiva's furious rage.

'Sati, my love. Why have you done this? Why did you give up your life for these worthless beings?' the great lord wept like a child.

Then he turned his ravaged, tear-stained face towards Daksha. 'You have killed my wife. I will not let you escape. I will destroy everyone present here. My beloved Sati has gone and nobody will be allowed to live,' he thundered. He began to spin like a tornado, dismembering Sati's body.

Shiva continued to dance his dance of destruction. He cut off Daksha's head but when Daksha's wife implored him to forgive her husband, he replaced it with a goat's head. 'Now you can be as vain and pompous as you wish,' he said.

Shiva, crazed with the loss of Sati, continued to howl as he ran around, leaving a trail of destruction in his path. His anguish, his intense grief and his rage grew stronger and stronger, creating an upheaval in all the three worlds. The gods and goddesses looked down, shocked and bewildered, as all of heaven trembled with fear. They exclaimed, 'What will happen now? Shiva's fury is going to destroy us all!'

Creating chaos in their wake, Shiva and his demons trampled all over the earth. Shiva carried Sati's body, calling out her name over and over again. 'Where are you, my beloved? Why have you left me? I will destroy everyone on this earth till you come back to me,' he shouted, his voice broken with grief, echoing all over the universe.

As Shiva strode from place to place, not caring where he was going, his mind deranged by his intense grief, one by one, all the body parts of Sati fell on to the earth. As soon as they touched the earth, a shrine rose at once in her memory.

Finally, there was nothing left of Sati's body and Shiva awoke as if from a terrible nightmare. He looked around, his eyes swollen with tears and saw he was not at home in Mount Kailash, where he and his beloved wife Sati had lived in such harmony and bliss. Shiva gazed up at the snowcapped mountains, weeping quietly, his body exhausted and covered with bleeding cuts and wounds.

Then a great silence fell as Lord Shiva sat down to meditate. The world now stood still. Shiva went into a hidden space in his mind and saw with his third eye that before she had given up her life, Sati had called out his name. 'I am your wife for eternity, my lord. You shall always be my husband in every life of mine.'

Shiva uttered her name over and over again and then slowly, breath by breath, Sati's name seeped into his being. She became a part of him. Shiva shut out the world that had taken Sati away from him and now concentrated only on her. Centuries passed as he sat in deep meditation on the lonely

Mount Kailash. Time ceased, the wind and the sun too stood still. The gods watched in despair.

'How will this end?' they wondered.

Then one day a glimmer of joy rippled through earth. The skies began to smile with relief. Sati was reborn on a remote mountain peak in the Himalayas. She was now Parvati and one day she would become Shiva's beloved wife once again. Their eternal love would make the world spin around once more with joy and harmony. The three worlds would rejoice in their everlasting love and celebrate this divine union forever.

4

SAVITRI & SATYAVAN

Love Conquers Death

'Earth sighs,
Sky sings,
Smudge-fire clouds,
Thick blanket of soft grass.
Yes,
Now is the time to be with
Your beloved
Now is the time to embrace.
And those whose lovers are not
With them
Call softly to death.'

—Vijjaka

Savitri was born as a gift from the gods. When she came of age, she was considered not only the most beautiful woman of the realm but also the most intelligent and learned. Her father, the king of Madra, had done years of penance and finally received a boon from the gods—a lovely girl was born in the palace at last. As she grew up, Savitri studied philosophy, music and astronomy and soon became well versed in many other subjects too. Though famed and admired all over the kingdom for her exquisite beauty and immense learning, Savitri was not married even after she came of age. Many royal suitors longed to be wed to her but they were too much in awe of this beautiful, highly intelligent woman and were afraid to ask for her hand in marriage. 'We are not good enough for this gorgeous maiden. She seems like a goddess from heaven. She has the beauty of Goddess Laxmi and the learning of Goddess Saraswati. How can we, humble mortals, ask for her hand?' they said, looking crestfallen whenever they caught sight of her. Savitri's father waited for some courageous prince to come forward and wed his beloved daughter but after a few years, he gave up all hope.

'I have decided that you should select your own husband. You must travel through the land and choose the right man for yourself. I have full faith in your superior judgement, my daughter,' he said to her one day.

Savitri, very pleased with her father's decision, set off at once in a fine chariot, accompanied by a large entourage. She travelled through cities, visited hermitages and also lived in many forest dwellings; she went up mountain paths and passed through countless villages, yet she did not find a man she wanted to wed.

She saw rich, handsome men, noble princes, brave warriors and met a few learned suitors too, but Savitri's heart would not accept any one of them.

She continued her search for that elusive, perfect husband because deep in her heart, she knew he was waiting for her somewhere. 'I will find my soulmate one day. I do not care how long it takes,' she said to herself every day.

Months passed and then one day she was passing thought a dense forest when she saw an incredibly handsome young man sitting under the shade of a tree. He was dressed simply in an ascetic's white robes but he did not seem like an ascetic. Tall, strong and handsome, he looked more like a proud warrior prince.

The moment she set eyes on him, Savitri knew he was the right man for her; he was the husband for whom she had been searching. 'At last, I have found him,' she said, her heart beating with joy. Then, for a moment, she felt a slight shiver of nervousness that ruined her happy mood. 'I hope he is not an ascetic or a married man.'

She sent her ministers to find out at once who the young man was and what he was doing all alone in the forest. They soon came back and told her that his name was Satyavan and though he was dressed like a hermit, he was a prince. His father, the king of Salva, had lost his kingdom when he became blind and now he lived in the forest with his wife and son. 'People say that Satyavan, a very devoted son, is considered the noblest and bravest of all men in this realm,' the minister said.

Savitri hurried back to her father and told him about her decision to marry Satyavan. The king was surprised and not very pleased at his daughter's decision.

'His father has lost his kingdom. Satyavan lives in a hut in the forest with his blind father and mother. He is a prince but destitute. He has no palace to live in, no armies to protect him and nobody to serve him. How can you, a royal princess, be happy with such a man? How will you endure the hardships of a forest life?' asked the king.

'He is poor and lives a simple life in the forest but he is the right man for me. I have made up my mind, father. Please give me your blessings,' she replied.

The king tried very hard to make his daughter change her mind but Savitri was firm in her resolve to marry Satyavan. While they were arguing about this topic, the ministers came and announced that Sage Narada had come to visit the king.

'O! We must go and welcome him,' said the king, and hurried out.

Sage Narada knew at once that the king was perturbed about something. When asked, the king told him that his beautiful, learned daughter wanted to marry a poor man living in the forest. 'His name is Satyavan.'

Narada nodded his head and smiled. 'Satyavan is the noblest of all men. He is radiant as the sun and as intelligent as Brhaspati. He is as valiant as Indra and as patient as the earth.'

The king was pleased to hear this but then he saw Sage Narada hesitate.

'There is only one thing,' said the sage in a voiced filled with sadness.

'What is it? What is the fault you are not telling me?' asked the king, looking at the sage anxiously.

'Satyavan has no faults.'

'Then why do you hesitate, great sage? ' asked the king.

'I hesitate to tell you the truth.'

'What is it? I know he is poor, he has lost his kingdom and lives in the forest with his blind father. But you said he is a noble and brave young man and my daughter seems to want only him. What more do I need to know?' asked the king.

'I must tell you that Satyavan will die within one year. He has only twelve months left to live. Your daughter will become a widow after only one year of her marriage,' said the sage.

The king, speechless with shock, stood quietly looking at Savitri, tears welling up in his eyes. 'What a terrible fate. What should they do now?'

Savitri had heard everything that Narada had said and now spoke in a quiet but firm voice. 'Respected sage and my beloved father. I have made up my mind to marry Satyavan. Nothing will make me change my mind. If he has only one year left to live, then we will live happily together for that one year given to us.'

The king, though sad and miserable, had no choice but to allow Savitri to marry her chosen groom. After the wedding, Savitri and Satyavan went to the forest to live with his parents. As soon as Savitri reached the small hut where they were going to live, she discarded all her fine royal robes and ornaments and dressed herself in a simple saree.

The days passed by swiftly. Savitri was happy living in the forest with her husband, whom she came to love and respect with all her heart. 'He is the perfect husband for me. I am grateful to the gods for giving him to me,' she thought.

Satyavan too loved her with all his heart. 'I am so fortunate to have you as my wife. You are a gem of a woman, so beautiful and wise. I will love you till I die,' he said, gently caressing her hands—now rough and scarred with hard work.

Though a royal princess, Savitri did all the humble chores in the hut and took great care of Satyavan's blind father and his aging mother. Only when darkness fell on the forest and all was still and silent would she think about the terrible threat hanging over Satyavan's head.

Death was waiting just around the corner to take him away from her.

As each day passed, she tried her best not to think about that terrible day that was to come and did all that she could to make Satyavan's life happy and joyous. She tried to live life to the fullest since she knew she had very few months left with her beloved husband.

Almost a year had passed and the day of Satyavan's death was fast approaching. Savitri stopped eating three days before the fateful, dark day. On the last night of Satyavan's life, she stayed awake all night praying and when dawn came, she woke up her husband.

'I will come with you to the forest today. I want to be with you,' she said.

Satyavan was surprised since she had never done this before but he allowed her to come with him. He picked up his axe and together they walked into the forest. After they had gathered some fruits and herbs, Savitri rested under a tree while Satyavan began to chop wood.

Within a few minutes, Satyavan began to sweat profusely. 'My head is aching terribly,' he cried and then stumbled. Savitri caught her husband as he was about to fall and laid him down on her lap. Her heart was beating with fear and waves of dread filled her entire body. She knew this was the fatal moment. He was about to die. Only a few breaths were left in his body.

Then she looked up. A huge, powerful man dressed in a shimmering, red robe was standing in front of her husband's lifeless body. He held a long rope in his massive hands.

'Who are you, my lord? Why have you come here?' asked Savitri in a polite voice.

'I am Yama, the god of death. I have come to take you husband's soul,' he said in a loud, booming voice.

The leaves on the tree began to shiver and an eerie darkness fell on them but Savitri was no longer afraid. 'I was told that you sent your messengers, my lord, to take souls away,' said Savitri, her head bowed.

'I do. But Satyavan is a noble, pure soul with an ocean of good qualities, so I have come to fetch him myself,' he said. He threw the rope around Satyavan's body and swiftly caught his soul. Then the god of death began walking away, taking giant strides. Savitri got up at once and started following him.

He could hear her footsteps behind them. 'Go back, woman. You cannot come with me. Go and prepare for your husband's funeral,' said Yama, not looking back.

'I mean no disrespect, my lord, but I will come with you to wherever you are taking my husband. It is a wife's duty.

In life and in death I am wedded to him. Please know that I have merits of prayer, devotion to elders and true love for my husband. I have also walked more than seven steps with you so I know now that I have your goodwill too,' said Savitri.

Yama was surprised but he was also impressed with Savitri's fearless reply.

'Ask for any boon you wish except for your husband's life. Then you must go back. You have come as far as you can with me. Take this boon from me and leave us,' he said, walking faster. He knew this was the only way to send the young girl back but Savitri kept following him.

'Please, great god of death, restore my father-in-law's sight,' she said.

Yama granted her wish swiftly, hoping the persistent girl would leave. But Savitri continued to follow him.

'Ask for one more boon and then go back, woman,' said Yama in an irritated voice.

Savitri asked for her father-in-law's kingdom to be returned to him.

Yama granted her this boon and said, 'Now you must return at once and begin the funeral rites for your dead husband. Go back, at once. I command you.'

But Savitri continued to follow him.

'I will grant you one last boon and after that you have to go back. You can come no further with me,' roared Yama, anger rising in his huge red eyes.

'Please grant me a boon that I may have a hundred sons from my husband,' said Savitri, bowing to the god of death.

'So be it,' said Yama, wanting to get rid of the girl.

'I thank you, my lord, with all my heart but how will I have a hundred sons when you are taking my husband away with you?' she asked in a quiet voice.

Yama knew when he was defeated and began to laugh. He had never met a woman on earth like this one. Pleased with Savitri's love and devotion to her husband, the god of death returned Satyavan's soul to her. 'May you live a hundred years with your husband,' he said and vanished into thin air, his laughter still echoing in the darkness.

Savitri rushed back to where she had left Satyavan. He was lying on the ground, his face pale and lifeless. As she watched anxiously, his inert body slowly came to life and he sat up rubbing his eyes. Savitri's eyes filled with tears of gratitude to the lord of death. He had been true to his word and returned her husband's life to her. She had managed to bring him back from the land of the dead. Savitri's heart filled with love and joy as she sat quietly watching her husband.

'Was I asleep for a long time? How dark it has become. We must go home now. Father and mother will be worried,' he said, looking up at her.

Slowly they made their way home in the dim moonlight. They could barely see the forest path and Satyavan was afraid they would get lost. At last, they reached the little hut and they heard loud voices ringing out in the darkness.

Satyavan's parents cried with relief as soon as they saw that the couple had returned safely from the forest and Satyavan was amazed to see his father had regained his sight.

As they were celebrating this miracle, a few soldiers came riding through the dark forest.

'Your majesty. The enemy has been defeated. You have regained your kingdom,' they announced.

Savitri smiled quietly as her husband and her father-in-law greeted this news with delight. 'The lord of death had kept all his promises. A hundred sons will be born to me and I will have a hundred years of wedded life to look forward to,' she thought to herself. She thanked Yama again in her heart as she looked at the fiery, red sun rising on the horizon. 'You have given us a new day and a new life to cherish, my lord,' said Savitri, her beautiful face glowing in the golden rays of dawn. She did not know that for countless centuries to come, her name—Sati Savitri—would symbolize a devoted, loving wife.

5

DRAUPADI & BHEEMA

An All-Consuming Love

'I search,
I fancy to see your body in the flowering creepers,
Your glances in the eyes of a startled deer,
The beauty of your face in the moon,
Your hair in the plumage of the peacock.
And the playful movements of your eyebrows
In the gentle ripples of the river.
But, O my beloved, nowhere does
Your likeness exist.
I search, endlessly.'

—Kalidasa, Meghaduta

He felt as though he were struck by a bolt of lightning the first time he saw her, and his heart began to race as if he were a young lad and not Bheema, the mighty warrior, a man who was famous all over the world for his incredible strength. As he gazed upon her exquisite face, he knew, deep in his heart, that she would never love him, yet he could not help falling head over heels in love with her.

Bheema and his brothers had just brought Draupadi from her swayamvar, fighting off a horde of furious princes and kings who were outraged that a Brahmin had won the lovely Princess Draupadi's hand. Bheema had stood firmly behind his brother Arjuna and together they had battled their way through, fearlessly pushing back their attackers.

When they reached home, their mother Kunti, not knowing that Arjuna had won himself a bride, commanded them to share whatever they had brought home. Draupadi now belonged to all five of them but Bheema could see clearly, from that very first day, that her heart would always belong to Arjuna. Arjuna was the chosen one for Draupadi and no one else. Her lovely eyes filled with adoration and longing each time she looked at Arjuna and when Bheema saw that loving gaze, he was filled with a deep ache that burned within him like a smouldering ember.

Bheema hoped that one day Draupadi would turn her beautiful, dark eyes towards him and say that she cared for him too. 'Bheema!' he often heard her voice in his head at night as he lay unhappy and sleepless. 'I love you. Come let us go away together.' But he knew this was not possible. All he could do was adore her from afar, quietly and furtively like a thief. Though he loved his brother Arjuna dearly, he could not help feeling jealous whenever he saw Arjuna and Draupadi together. He waited patiently, standing in the shadows, praying and hoping for a loving glance or a kind word from her.

Draupadi did turn to him but only to ask him to kill for her—not once but many times—and he gladly soaked his hands in blood just to please her. It gave his lovesick heart solace when he saw her triumphant glance; when she smiled at him each time he took revenge on her behalf.

Draupadi's thirst for revenge knew no boundaries and her temper was always balancing on the edge of a sword. 'She was born from a sacred fire and thus has a fiery temper. We must be careful never to annoy her or upset her,' their eldest brother Yudhishthira often said, but he did not add how difficult her life had been ever since she had married the five of them.

From the day she came to live with them—a young princess, sheltered and indulged by her father, the king Drupada, she had known nothing but hardship. She roamed with them in the forest, dressed in frayed clothes, foraging for food. 'I cannot bear the despair raging within me when I see her plight,' Bheema said to himself. He thought his heart would break each time he saw Draupadi dressed in rags, sleeping on the hard ground surrounded by wild, thorny plants. He tried very hard to make her more comfortable by bringing her soft grass to lie on or by carrying her in his arms when she was too tired to walk, but he had to be careful of showing her too much attention. He was afraid his mother Kunti would reprimand him because she wanted Draupadi to be treated like everyone else.

'She is the love of my life. I cannot see her suffer. I must help her somehow. But what can I do? How can I take her away from this wretched life? She is a princess and she must live in a palace. My heart bleeds when I see her tender feet cut and bruised by stones when she walks on these rough forest paths,' cried Bheema in anger. 'We are trapped in destiny's web and will never escape from this terrible life till fate decides to do something in our favour. My hands are tied for thirteen years while we are in exile. My powerful body and immense strength are of no use to my beloved Draupadi, the princess I adore with all my sorrow-laden heart.'

Bheema often roamed the forest at night, his head reeling with the horrifying image of Dushasana pulling Draupadi's saree, trying to disrobe her. He could not forget how he and his four brothers had sat silently in mortification and watched their wife being humiliated, and how they could not do anything to save her since they were all slaves now that Yudhishthira had lost them in a game of dice against the Kauravas. How his blood had boiled with rage as he had stood, helpless and ashamed, while his beloved Draupadi begged for help. Krishna had come to Draupadi's rescue and made the saree endless and so Dushasana finally had to give up. But Bheema could never forgive himself for not going to help her. 'Listen to me, Dushasana. I will tear your heart from your body and drink your blood. This I vow to do and may I never reach the heavens after I die if I don't fulfill my oath,' he had shouted.

Then Duryodhana, the eldest Kaurava, had laughed loudly and leered at Draupadi. 'Come, Panchali. Come and sit on my lap,' he had said, slapping his thighs as the elders gathered at the assembly watched silently in shame and horror.

Bheema remembered how he had roared, his entire body shaking helplessly, tears running down his cheeks. He had raised a massive clenched fist and threatened Duryodhana. 'I swear that I will break your thighs, you vile creature, or else I will never attain my rightful place in heaven,' he had shouted, his voice hoarse with rage. He whispered that vow again in the forest, his angry words hissing in the darkness like sparks from a huge fire.

'I love her more than my life. Is that why I feel her pain, her hurt, more than the others? Does Arjuna love her as much as I do or is he indifferent to her? I know that he is the most important person in her life besides Krishna. Will she ever love me as much as I love her? Will she ever love me as much as she loves Arjuna?' he asked himself, gazing at the sleeping figure of Draupadi. 'Not in this lifetime,' a voice whispered in his head.

'I should be content by just loving her. It is not important that she returns my love; I should be content just to gaze upon her beautiful face and hear her voice. It does not matter that she is not mine alone. I am happy to get a little portion of her exquisite being,' he repeated to himself.

No one ever knew how much he suffered because he took great care to stay calm and impassive in her presence. Bheema waited, praying that the day would come soon when he could fulfill the vows he had made so long ago. Then he would show Draupadi how much he loved and cherished her. He would avenge each insult, each word of disrespect that she had had to suffer. They had been in exile for more than ten years now and only three more remained.

'Soon, my love, soon I will win your heart by avenging every cruel deed that has been heaped upon your pure, noble self.' The dark, lonely nights in the forest seemed endless and thoughts of revenge were constantly on his mind. Draupadi would come and sit by him sometimes and together they would dream of the day the blood of the Kauravas would spill on the earth.

'If my brother Yudhishthira had not bound us with these ropes of slavery and banishment, no man alive would ever dare to touch a hair on your head. Let them wait. I will kill each one of them. Only for now we have to wander in this forest like hunted animals,' he said to her, his eyes blazing with fury. Draupadi smiled and touched his hand. Bheema at once felt as if a ripple of cool water had swept over him, calming his fevered body. He wanted to take her in his arms but hesitated. This was not the year he could be with her. Each of the five brothers had been given a year with Draupadi and Bheema had to wait for his turn. 'I wonder if she ever thinks of me or even wants to be with me. I know from the way she sighs all the time that she longs for Arjuna to come back to her. She does not care that he has married another woman. Arjuna and only Arjuna will always be her true beloved husband,' thought Bheema, his heart aching with a heavy sadness. He knew this longing and pain would never leave him till he died.

'I know how impatient you are. I feel the same way but I know our time to take revenge will come one day. And I know you will always be there for me,' said Draupadi.

'I promise you, my love, my wife, I will avenge every insult you have had to suffer in this life. You will have your wish and wash your hair in Dushasana's blood,' said Bheema, tears of quiet rage welling up in his eyes.

'If only my Lord Yudhisthira would send you to kill Duryodhana and Dushasana. I know you can easily do this,' said Draupadi, giving him a quick glance.

'I know my brother well. His sense of righteousness will never allow him to break any rules. We have had to endure this exile for twelve years. Now only one year is left and then we can we take our revenge,' said Bheema, trying to quieten the rage simmering within him. Draupadi continued to stare at him, her eyes sad and hurt, and Bheema walked away, looking like a chained lion who could not attack his prey.

Months passed slowly and one day, Bheema and Draupadi were walking in the forest. A cool breeze touched Draupadi's face. It carried the heady scent of a strange flower. 'This must be the "saugandhika" flower. They say its scent never fades,' cried Draupadi in delight. Bheema, happy to see her so pleased, promised he would fetch her these fragrant blossoms.

The next day he set out at dawn in search of the flowers. He looked for them everywhere, following the trail of the strong perfume, going deeper and deeper into the forest till he was quite lost. The scent kept getting stronger till he finally came upon a river where there were thousands of these fragrant blossoms floating in the sparkling waters. 'This seems like an enchanted forest so I must be careful. But I must get the flowers for Draupadi,' thought Bheema. However, as soon as he began plucking the flowers, a team of rakshashas leapt upon him.

'Stop! How dare you steal flowers from the river? These belong to King Kubera,' they shouted, trying to force him back.

Bheema laughed and said, 'My wife Draupadi wants these flowers and I will get them for her. Stop me if you dare.'

The rakshasas began howling furiously and attacked him as soon as he spoke these words but Bheema killed them all with his bare hands. When Kubera was told that a human being had entered the river like a wild elephant, the king smiled and said, 'That must be Bheema. Let him take the saugandhika flowers for his wife Draupadi, whom he loves so passionately.'

Draupadi was very pleased when Bheema placed a hundred scented flowers in her lap and she gently placed her hands on his arm, to thank him. Bheema's heart leapt with joy. His bruised, bleeding hands and his battle-weary body seemed to recover as if by magic when Draupadi smiled at him, her beautiful face glowing with happiness as she inhaled the heady scent of the flowers. 'She does love me a little. I can see it in her eyes,' thought Bheema.

'I will take you one day to the scented garden and we will sit by the river, just the two of us,' he whispered. Draupadi, busy caressing the scented flowers, did not answer him. How he longed for a little time with her alone. 'I will ask her tomorrow. She will certainly say yes to me,' he thought, a deep feeling of happiness flowing over him like a soothing balm.

But his joy did not last long. The next day at dawn, they heard a thundering sound and the sky was suddenly aglow with a strange unearthly light. A bedecked chariot began to descend to the ground. 'It is Arjuna,' cried Draupadi, running towards the chariot, her long tresses flying, her arms outstretched. Then, as Arjuna stepped down, she stood very still, looking at him as if she were seeing him for the first time. Bheema saw her face light up as if touched by the golden glow of the dawn and he turned his face away. Envy, tinged with sorrow, flooded over him but he controlled himself and rushed forward to greet Arjuna, his brother whom he loved truly.

As their days of exile in the forest continued, Bheema often sat quietly watching Draupadi as she went about doing her chores. He felt sorry for her and tried to help her when Kunti was not watching. He would gather wood for her, search the forest for wild fruits and berries and fetch water for her. All night long he would stand guard when she slept. 'Does she ever think of me? I am sure she dreams of only Arjuna at night but maybe once in a while, her thoughts turn to me,' he thought, a forlorn hope rising and then subsiding in the core of his heart.

Bheema wanted desperately to share his innermost feelings with her though he was afraid she might laugh at him. One day, when he found her alone he could not stop himself from telling her how he felt.

'I love you like I have loved no other woman. I will aways be by your side. You can ask me to do anything for you,' he said to her, his words rushing out like a stream.

In response, she just smiled quietly. 'I know that. I can always depend on you, my brave husband. You are not like Arjuna, who has married so many women and broken my heart,' she said, her eyes searching for Arjuna, who had wandered away as usual.

Bheema ignored the dart of envy that stabbed him once again. 'I will accept that she only loves Arjuna but I will continue to love her all my life,' he said to himself. And somehow these words, once spoken aloud, made him feel happier.

'You can ask me to do anything for you. I will even give my life for you,' he said to Draupadi, and she turned and gave him a tender look that thrilled him to the core.

Then soon a day arrived when Bheema could prove the words he had spoken to Draupadi were true. All the five brothers had gone out to hunt, leaving Draupadi alone in the hut, when a king called Jayadratha happen to pass by in his chariot. He saw Draupadi standing under a tree, her dark tresses gleaming in the sunlight, and he fell madly in love with her. He did not know who she was, he only knew that she was the most beautiful woman he had ever seen. 'What are you doing in this forest all by yourself? Come away with me, beautiful lady. I will make you my queen,' he said.

Draupadi gave him an angry glance and walked away. Though she did not show her fear, she was afraid since her husbands were out in the forest and she was all alone in the hut.

'Go away from here before my husbands catch you and kill you. Bheema, my husband, is a most ferocious and powerful man and he will not spare your life if he sees you anywhere near me,' she said loudly, trying not to sound afraid.

'You are so lovely, just like a heavenly maiden. I cannot let you go, my dark, beautiful one. I have to make you mine,' said Jayadratha and, swiftly picking her up in his arms, he strode back to his chariot.

Far away in the forest, Bheema suddenly felt something was not right. His brother Yudhishthira, too, saw an evil omen gleaming in the sky and they decided to rush back to the hut. When they found out what had happened to Draupadi, Bheema gave a cry of despair that echoed all through the forest . 'How dare he? I will kill him,' he yelled, crashing his fists into a tree trunk.

'Let us chase after him. He could not have gone far with her. We will catch him,' said Arjuna, and both the brothers ran, following the trail left by the chariot wheels. They soon caught up with the king and in a flash of a moment they overpowered him. Bheema set Draupadi free and then he turned to face the king, growling with rage. He rammed his fists into the king's face and then he put his massive hands around his neck and was about to kill him when he heard Yudhishthira's voice calling out to him. 'Spare him, Bheema. Jayadratha is married to our sister Dushala. We cannot make her a widow. You have punished him enough. Let him go now.'

Bheema held the king's throat in his powerful hands and began squeezing the breath out of him. 'I cannot let him live. He has dared to touch Draupadi. He must die,' roared Bheema.

With great difficulty, Arjuna pulled him away from the king.

'Yudhishthira has told us that we cannot kill him. We cannot disobey our brother. Let's drag this wretch with us and make him beg for Draupadi's forgiveness,' said Arjuna, trying to calm Bheema.

Bheem let go of the fallen king reluctantly. He spat on him and said, 'You will come with us. You will touch your head to Draupadi's feet and declare yourself her slave.'

Jayadratha heaved a sigh of relief and followed them to the hut. Bheema kicked him forward and forced him to bow to Draupadi. Her eyes blazing with anger, she looked down at the king cowering at her feet. 'I will be you slave forever. Forgive me,' he cried. She turned her face away. Bheema could see the disappointment in her eyes. He knew that she would have been happier if he had killed this man who had dared to molest her. Once again, he had been restrained by his brother Yudhishthira, and he knew that Draupadi was as unhappy as him to let this vile man live.

'I will guard you day and night,' he whispered, but Draupadi walked away. She seemed to have lost all her faith in him and Bheema hid his face in his hands and sobbed like a child. 'What can I do? How shall I keep her safe?' he said over and over again.

Another year of hardship and despair passed. Now the five Pandava brothers and Draupadi were living in King Virata's palace in disguise and only fifteen days were left of their banishment when Draupadi became a victim of a man's lust again. As soon as Kichaka, the queen's brother, saw Draupadi, who was now disguised as a humble serving girl, he desperately wanted this dark beauty. 'Send that girl to my chamber,' he commanded. When Draupadi refused, the queen scolded her and forced her to go to her brother since she did not want to displease the commander of the king's army.

Draupadi managed to saved her herself and went running to Bheema, who was now working as a cook in the palace kitchen. 'You are the only one who can save me,' she cried, falling at his feet. 'You must kill that evil Kichaka and save me from his vile lust. If you don't kill him I will kill myself,' she sobbed.

Bheema picked her up and held her trembling body in his arms, gently caressing her. 'I will. I promise you, my wife, I will kill him tonight,' he whispered. 'This time I will not listen to Yudhishthira.' That night, Bheema stole into Kichaka's bedchamber and strangled him with his bare hands. He broke his limbs and torso into pieces and even after Kichaka was dead, Bheema continued to pound him, as if he were taking out thirteen years of helpless rage. Finally, he threw away what remained of Kichaka's body and turned to face Draupadi. He had never seen her look so happy in years.

'You are the only one of my husbands who truly loves me,' said Draupadi, throwing her arms around Bheema and holding him close to her. She gently touched his face and kissed him on his lips passionately as she had never done before.

'At last she belongs to me. At this moment when my hands are covered in blood, she truly loves me more than Arjuna,' thought Bheema as he shut his eyes in ecstasy.

Then, an uneasy feeling of dread crept into his heart. He suddenly saw the bloodshed that was to come.

It was only at this moment in time that Draupadi belonged to him as never before. 'My loyal husband Bheema. You are always there for me and that is why I always come to you for help. I love you,' she whispered, her dark eyes glinting, not with love but with triumph. But her words were enough for Bheema. He would cherish them to last him a lifetime. He would kill for Draupadi over and over again and he would love this woman till he died. One day, he hoped, she could truly love him too.

6

PARVATI & SHIVA

Divine and Passionate Love

'When with her lotus eyes on her mirror,
She saw the reflection of her radiant loveliness,
Swift
She hastened to seek Shiva,
For the essence of a woman's being
Is the light in
The lover's eye.'

—Kalidas, Kumārasambhava

A gentle breeze carried the scent of magnolia blossoms all over the hillside. Ivory white clouds chased each other as they played hide and seek with the sun. Parvati gazed up at the high, snow-capped mountain peaks and her heart was filled with longing. Her eyes glistened with tears as she looked up at her beloved Lord Shiva who sat meditating, oblivious of her presence.

'Oh! Why are you so distant? Why don't you open your brilliant eyes and look at me, my lord? Just once, look at me and you will see how my entire being longs for you. Give me only a brief moment and you will see how my love for you shines in my eyes,' cried Parvati, but the breeze carried her words away.

Shiva continued to sit absolutely still on the highest mountain peak, his white body gleaming like a snow-covered rock. He was dressed in frayed animal skins and his body was covered in ashes—yet in Parvati's eyes he was the most handsome man she had ever seen. Shiva was the only one for her and she prayed for him day and night.

Parvati, was the daughter of Himavat, the king of the high mountains and her mother was the beautiful apsara Menaka. From the time Parvati was a young girl, she knew that she was destined to marry the great God Rudra one day. Her parents had chosen him for her but, however much they tried, Shiva would not come out of his deep meditation. Parvati had been his wife in her last life but, tragically, she had taken her own life, since she could not bear to see her husband being insulted by her father. Shiva had never forgotten his beloved Sati and now, as years passed, he sat quietly in a deep meditation that no one dared to disturb.

The beautiful Parvati had been chosen as the perfect wife for the god of destruction, and all the gods in heaven desperately wanted this marriage to happen as soon as possible. A terrible rakshasa called Taraka was wreaking havoc on heaven and earth and none could stop this powerful demon because he had been given a boon by Brahma and was now invincible. 'Only a son born to Shiva and Parvati will be able to kill this asura,' declared Brahma.

Parvati, with her graceful figure, sweet voice and lotus-eyes, was so lovely that all men lost the power of speech when they saw her. 'She will be Shiva's consort and their son will destroy Taraka and save us from total annihilation,' said the gods, pleased to have found a solution at last. 'Let them be married at soon as possible,' they declared happily. But however much everyone wanted this perfect match between Shiva and Parvati, it was not going to according to plan.

Shiva sat still like a giant rock on his remote mountain peak. Parvati's unmatched loveliness and her graceful, exquisite figure had no effect on the great lord of destruction. Shiva would not open his eyes and look at her. Parvati waited and waited for him to show the slightest sign that he had noticed her but his handsome face was forever still. His brilliant eyes were always shut and even his breathing was barely visible. It seemed to Parvati as if he were carved out of granite. He refused to open his eyes even though Parvati sat near his feet for hours. Her heart was filled with sadness and her lovely eyes glistened with tears as she gazed upon her lord.

'Why does he not open his eyes and look at me? Even one brief glance from his diamond eyes will fill me with so much joy. Look at me, O lord. I beseech you,' Parvati lay her head down on the grass and wept quietly. The high mountain peaks, the clouds floating in the sky and the birds and animals in the forest all watched the beautiful girl as she lay on the grass, her face drenched with tears, and they all felt the deep sorrow churning in her heart. But they were all helpless. Even Himavat and Menaka could not help their daughter. The gods watched from heaven, wondering what to do now.

Shiva was a most formidable god and no one dared approach him as he sat meditating. How could the marriage of Shiva and Parvati take place if he would not even look at her? The gods began to get really worried since the demon Taraka was threatening to overthrow their kingdom in heaven. Indra was about to lose his throne. 'What can we do to break Shiva's meditation? Whom can we ask for help?' they wondered. Then Indra suddenly thought of Kama, the god of love.

'Let us call Kama. He is the only one who can help us. He will send a dart of love from his bow.' Thrilled with this plan, the gods rushed to Kama and told him to go to the mountain peak where Shiva sat meditating. Kama agreed at once and, gathering up his bow and arrow of blossoms, he flew to the mountains.

When Kama saw Shiva's great, white figure garlanded with snakes, seated on the mountain peak, he suddenly faltered. He felt his love dart might not have any effect on such a great, powerful god. The aura surrounding Shiva was like a streak of lightning. How could Kama's arrow pierce it? Then he saw a lovely girl walking on the hillside. She was the most beautiful girl he had ever seen and he knew, at once, that this must be Parvati.

'My love dart cannot fail now. It will work its magic as soon as the great Lord Shiva's gaze falls upon this exquisite maiden,' said Kama and, saying a quick prayer, he drew his bow. The love dart flew straight at Shiva and struck him between his brows.

For a moment there was utter silence. Then the earth began to shake and the mountains swayed as a frightening roll of thunder crashed in the sky. The gods held their breath in fear. What was happening? Lord Shiva had opened his third eye. Furious at being disturbed, he looked around and saw Kama. Shiva's third eye opened wider and it seemed the sky was suddenly aflame with his anger. Then a bolt of lightning flashed. It raced straight towards Kama, who had been hiding in the shadows, and burnt him to ashes. Within seconds, nothing remained of the unfortunate god of love except for a pile of ash. Shiva had not even glanced at Parvati who now lay at his feet, trembling with fear. She gave a loud cry and fainted.

When Parvati finally woke up, the sun was about to set behind the peaks. She glanced at the white, still figure as immobile as a rock and gave a cry of despair. 'He will never look at me. He will never love me in this life. All is lost now. I might as well give up my life,' she sobbed. Then she fell silent and looked at the snowy peaks beyond. She knew what she was going to do. Parvati slowly rose and started walking towards the dark forest. As she walked, she began to discard her jewellery and the ornaments in hair. Finally, dressed in only her saree, she sat down under a tree and began to meditate. 'I will undertake a severe penance on this mountain to win my great Lord Shiva. I will pray on his name for as long as there is breath in my body,' she said, and then did not utter a single word.

For many years, she sat alone in the forest, braving the cold fury of the mountains, the harsh winds and the blazing sun. She did not eat or take even a sip of water. Day and night, she sat there meditating and all the gods in heaven watched in awe. They began to call her Aparna—one who fasts and does not even eat leaves.

Years went by, Parvati sat alone, lost in prayers. Her only thought was Shiva. He was destined to be her husband—she knew that in her heart. When and how she did not know but she would continue to pray and worship him till she died. The trees in the forest and all the wild animals watched the frail girl as she sat alone. They tried to protect her as well as they could. Creepers grew near Parvati's feet and water from the rain gathered in pools all around her but she never noticed anything. Shiva was the only thought in her mind and she prayed for him with all her fading strength.

Then one day when the morning sun was gleaming on the snow-covered peaks and the breeze carried the faint scent of wild roses, Parvati heard footsteps. Startled, she opened her eyes. Who would come to this remote place in the mountains? The only living creatures she had seen for many years were deer, foxes and birds. Silence had been her only companion for decades and her eyes and ears had become so sensitive that she could even hear dewdrops falling on flower petals. The footsteps came closer but Parvati kept her eyes shut. She did not want to see anyone or talk to anyone. She was not going to break her meditation.

Parvati sat so still that a butterfly came and sat on her shoulders, gently fluttering its wings. The footsteps stopped. Parvati could sense the presence of this being very close to her. 'Who could it be?' she thought again. Pavati was not afraid of any danger to herself. Sitting alone in this lonely forest for years, she was not afraid of any living creature. Along with hunger and thirst, she had forgotten fear too. Wild animals roamed around her and snakes slithered past her feet but Parvati would not notice them.

The person now came closer to her. Parvati felt a strange, cool yet sharp light fall upon her closed eyelids and she reluctantly opened her eyes.

A tall man dressed in the robes of an ascetic stood before her. Parvati bowed her head to him silently.

'Who are you? You look like a maiden from a noble family. Why are you in this forest all alone?' he asked.

Parvati did not reply and continued to bow her head.

'Tell me, lovely young maiden, why are you doing such a severe penance? What do you wish to achieve with this hardship you have brought upon your body? I can see how fragile you are now with years of fasting. What do you desire?' asked the hermit.

Parvati looked up but still did not reply. She did not wish to offend this holy man but she could not bring herself to explain to him the reason she was all alone in this forest or why she was doing such a severe penance. She wished he would go away and leave her alone.

But the hermit kept looking at her with his piercing eyes. His eyes were like two brilliant jewels and Parvati could not look away. He smiled at her and said, 'Tell me the reason why you are doing such a difficult test and I will give you half the merit of my own penance and prayers of hundreds of years.'

Finally, Parvati spoke in a low voice. 'I am doing this meditation and penance to win the love of my Lord Shiva. I wish to marry him,' she said softly.

'Shiva? Why do you want to have anything to do with him? I have seen him. He covers his body with ashes. He wears only animal skins and he drapes snakes around his neck. How can a beautiful young girl like you become the bride of such an uncouth being?' said the hermit.

Parvati heard him speak and his words filled her with anger. She forced herself to remain silent. 'Please go away and leave me alone,' she said in her mind.

Then she realized the hermit could read her mind because he replied to her, 'I will go away but you should give up this penance and forget about Shiva. Give him up and chose someone more worthy of you. Shiva is poor and has no family to speak of; his only companions are wild animals and strange, ugly creatures. Shiva is not the bridegroom for you.'

Parvati could no longer control her anger. She turned to the hermit and spoke in a voice quivering with rage. 'Please do not speak such words about my Lord Shiva. It is a sin for me to listen to these cruel, harsh words about my beloved. I worship him. I adore him and I will continue to adore him till I die. I do not care that his body is covered with ashes. I do not care that he is poor and lives the life of a hermit. I love him above all. He is my chosen husband and I will continue to do penance till I win his love or I will give up this body of mine,' said Parvati as tears welled up in her lovely eyes.

The hermit stood very still and watched her, a strange smile playing on his gaunt face.

'Now, I beg you humbly and with respect to please go away and leave me alone,' said Parvati. She turned away and had just walked a few steps when the hermit came and stood before her. She moved and he moved with her, taking silent steps to match hers.

'Sir, let me pass,' said Parvati, getting more and more angry at this rude behavior. Why was this man tormenting her like this? Holy men did not behave in this manner. Who was he? Parvati began to run but however fast she ran, the hermit was just a step behind her. Breathless, angry and unable to tolerate it anymore, she shouted, 'I beg you. Please leave me alone.'

'Do you really want me to leave you alone, my beautiful Parvati?' a voice whispered close in her ears and Parvati stood still, frozen with shock.

The sky changed from grey to silver and before her stood the great Lord Shiva; her beloved Lord Shiva. His towering figure was engulfed in a brilliant light and his ash-covered body was gleaming like molten silver. Stunned to behold such a magnificent image of her lord, Parvati could not breathe. She closed her eyes and then quickly opened them again. Shiva continued to smile at her gently.

'Come to me, my love. You have won me over with your sincere devotion and your dedicated penance; your true meditation. You shall be my wife and I will love and cherish you forever,' he said as he reached out his hand to Parvati.

Thus the marriage of Shiva and Parvati was celebrated with great joy in heaven and on the sparkling mountain peaks. Gods as well as apsaras danced and celestial musicians played sweet music, which resounded all over the skies and blessed all those who were fortunate enough to hear it. Parvati was happy to be with her Lord Shiva at last. She often looked at him and wondered if this was a beautiful dream and she would wake up and find he was not there. But Shiva was always by her side, a loving, devoted husband and her love for him knew no bounds.

In a few years a son, Kartikeya, was born to them and he grew up to became the god of war. He challenged the demon Taraka who had been tormenting the gods and killed him. Peace and happiness were restored in heaven and on earth once more. Far away on the remote, snow-capped peaks, hidden by dancing clouds, Shiva and Parvati sat together with the light of their glorious, divine love shining over all three worlds for an eternity.

7

SITA & RAM

Love in Separation

'Blow wind, to where my love is
Touch her, and come and touch me soon,
I'll feel her gentle touch through you,
And meet her beauty in the moon,
These things are much for one who loves,
A man can live by them alone,
That she and I breathe the same air,
And the earth we tread is one.'

—Valmiki's Ramayana, Book 6, Chapter 5, Verse 6

The moon hid behind the clouds, casting dark shadows beneath the Asoka trees. Sita sat beneath them with her head bowed, and touched the torn petals of the flowers that had fallen near her feet. An overwhelming feeling of sadness flooded over her as she recalled Ram's voice calling out her name. She shut her eyes and his noble, handsome face rose before her. He was holding a garland of jasmine flowers and smiling as he came forward to weave the garland into her hair. 'Sita, my beloved wife,' he whispered gently as their hands touched.

Every morning, they had gathered flowers together from the plants that grew near their hut. The forest loomed just beyond, dark and full of hidden dangers, but Sita felt safe with Ram and his brother Laxman to guard her. What harm could ever come to her with these two warriors by her side?

Those peaceful, happy days seemed to have been lost in the mists of time. There was nothing but sorrow and grief for her now. Sita looked up at the Asoka trees swaying in the darkness. The demonesses guarding her snorted and laughed loudly as they mocked her. She, the wife of the prince of Ayodhya, Ram, was now a prisoner in the kingdom of Lanka. In one cruel stroke, using dark magic, Ravana had taken her away from her lord and destroyed her life.

Why was she being treated like this by fate? For what reason was she being punished? She had never harmed anyone. She had never said a cruel word to a single soul. Why had fate plunged her into these depths of despair? These questions plagued Sita as she sat imprisoned in the garden. 'Will I ever see my lord again? Will I ever hear his sweet voice again?' she cried.

'O gentle, sweetly scented breeze. Carry my message to Lord Ram. Tell him, "Sita is bereft without you. Her heart is broken and she calls out to you, day and night." Go breeze, tell him how I long for him,' she whispered to the swaying leaves.

Sita had followed Ram when he had been ordered by King Dasharatha to leave the comforts of the palace and live in the forest for fourteen years. As long as she was with her husband, she was content. She could face any hardship if she knew Ram was by her side.

Sita—a royal princess, quickly learnt to live like a forest maiden, surviving on wild fruit and sleeping on the rough ground. How happy she was in their little hut in the forest. Birds sang all day and deer came up to feed from her hands at their doorstep. Those days now seemed like a beautiful dream.

Now she was a prisoner in this arbour of Asoka trees, surrounded by ferocious demonesses, and her days were full of sadness and despair. Though the garden Ravanawas filled with beautiful flowering trees, and gold and silver fountains played music all day, her surroundings filled her with a terrible fear. She watched the moon fade away as the first rays of dawn streaked the sky. 'O silver-beamed moon! Why does Ram not come to rescue me? Has he forgotten about me? Can you see him and tell me how he fares without me?' Sita said, lifting her head to the sky, letting the tears stream down her face. Only crying made her heart feel less burdened by this terrible sadness. Tears were her only relief.

Every day, the king of Lanka came to visit her. He stood in front of her in his regal splendour, bedecked in dazzling jewels. 'You were meant for me, Sita. Your beauty was only made to match my greatness, my immense power. Forget about Ram. He is nothing but a helpless young boy compared to a mighty, powerful king like me. You will never see him again. Marry me, Sita. Together we will roam heaven and earth in my golden flying chariot. You will be my chief queen. You will have all the riches of this world.' And when she would decline, he would say, 'Why do you resist me, you proud, foolish girl? You have to give me your answer soon.

You have to become mine or I will kill you. I will feed your dead body to the lions.' Over and over, he repeated these terrible threats.

'Ram has been slayed by our great king,' chanted the demonesses guarding her. Their words filled her heart with terror.

'O gods in heaven. Please let that not be true. Take my wretched life instead and let him live,' Sita prayed continuously.

As the first rays of sunlight fell on the trees, Sita suddenly heard a faint sound and looked up. A tiny monkey, perched on the garden wall, was gazing at her with sparkling, intelligent eyes. He folded his paws and bowed to her. For a brief moment Sita was happy to see this clever-looking monkey but suddenly, she felt a dart of fear. Could this be another of Ravana's evil tricks to deceive her? Then the monkey bowed his head and began to sing Ram's praises in a soft, melodious voice. He narrated the sweet words in such an exquisite, pure language that Sita sat up at once to listen. She shut her eyes as the words in praise of her Lord Ram flowed like a cool, gentle stream, soothing her, calming her troubled soul. Finally, the monkey stopped chanting and came forward. He placed a signet ring in her hands and moved back. Sita's heart leapt with joy. It was Ram's ring. Could this be real? Or was she imagining it? Could her eyes—so tired and weary from endless sobbing—be deceiving her? She touched the ring with hesitant fingers and then pressed it to her eyes. Ram stood before her and in her mind's eye she saw him smiling at her. He was saying something to her. Sita sat very still, holding her breath, and listened as his beloved voice floated towards her. 'O, my beloved Sita. Where are you? I am heartbroken without your sweet presence. I search everywhere for you. I ask the sky, the trees and the birds to tell me if they have seen you. I am a lost soul. I find no peace when I cannot see you, my beloved wife.'

Tears of happiness began to flow down her cheeks and though she was filled with sadness and longing, Sita felt a brief moment of joy that caused her to tremble. Ram was alive. Ram had not forgotten her.

'You bring me a mingled draught of bliss and pain. Bliss that he wears me in his heart. Pain that he wakes and weeps apart,' she said softly to the monkey sitting near her feet.

'Maa Sita. I have flown over the ocean to bring you this message. Your Lord Ram loves you infinitely; he is desolate at being parted from you and thinks only of how to bring you back. He will be here soon. Be not afraid. He will come with a mighty army of monkeys and bears to rescue you. Till then he leads a life of sadness. He repeats your name over and over again and weeps when he thinks no one is watching him. He speaks to the trees and tells them, "Sita is to me what light is to the sun. We are inseparable. So why has she gone away?" Our Lord Ram is desolate without you, Maa Sita,' said the monkey, whose name Sita now knew, was Hanuman.

Sita did not know whether to feel happiness or sorrow when she heard these words. 'You speak of my lord's love for me and they fall on my ears like soft dew. They fill me with joy and yet when you speak of his grief, his sadness, your words are like drops of bitter poison to me, Hanuman, my son. Why has cruel fate separated us? What harm have we ever done to anyone to deserve this fate?' she said.

Hanuman tried to console her and told her that her days of sorrow would soon be over. 'I will race back to Lord Ram and tell him that I have seen you, but what sign shall I carry to show him that I met you and spoke to you? My humble plea is that I carry you back to him on my shoulders across the ocean,' said Hanuman, pleased with himself to have thought of such a clever plan.

'No, Hanuman. That is not right. My lord must come and rescue me. He will fight for my honour. That is the correct way. I will not steal back like a thief. I will return to my lord only when he comes himself to take me,' said Sita, holding back her tears. She then asked Hanuman to come and sit by her.

'I shall now tell you a few details of our life together that only we both know. That will convince him that you have met me. I shall also give you this jewel given to me at my wedding to Lord Ram,' said Sita. She untied a knot at the corner of her saree and gave Hanuman a small jewel she had kept concealed within it. Then in a low, soft voice, she began telling Hanuman about her life with Ram.

As she spoke, visions of her happy life with Ram came flooding back to her and her eyes again filled with tears. How long ago it all seemed! She recalled walking in the dense forest of Chitrakoot with her husband. 'The sun was strong and it was hot even in the shade. We soon got tired and sat down in a grassy meadow. Ram lay his head on my lap and fell asleep. A few minutes later a crow swooped down and pecked at my bosom with its sharp beak. I threw a pebble at it to chase it away but it kept coming back to attack me. I tried not to cry but the pain was unbearable. Ram soon woke up and saw what had happened. At first, he was amused and laughed at me but when he saw the bruise the crow's beak had made on my skin, he was shocked.

He quickly soothed my skin with his tender touch and the pain disappeared at once. Then he swiftly sent an arrow from his quiver towards the crow. The bird was an asura and it quickly fell at Ram's feet to beg his pardon.

Repeat to my lord every word I tell you, Hanuman. Tell him this also: one morning when I was tired and hot under the noonday sun, my red bindi was wiped off by perspiration. My husband playfully took some red dust from a rock and applied it on my forehead with his noble hands. Remind him of those blissful days we spent in Chitrakoot. O, Hanuman. Tell I cannot wait much longer. Tell him to come and save me.'

After Hanuman left the grove, Sita sat quietly for a long time, thinking about her life. The demonesses who guarded her seemed to have gone to sleep when Sita had been talking to Hanuman. She was thankful to be left alone for a while and cried softly to ease her aching heart. All around her the Asoka trees swayed and murmured as if they understood her grief. They cast their deep, green shade on her like a soothing balm.

Sita had never thought life would plunge her into such depths of sorrow. She felt a brief moment of joy as she remembered how she had fallen in love with Ram as soon as she had set eyes on him through a lattice window at her father's palace. He shone like a brilliant jewel amongst that gathering of princes. He was dressed simply yet he looked like the noble prince that he was. How fortunate she was to marry him! She had felt blessed by the gods in heaven. They had spent a brief joyous time in Ayodhya, living in the splendour and comfort of the palace before dark clouds began to gather. When Ram had been banished by his father King Dasharatha to go and live in the forest for fourteen years, Ram did not want Sita to go with him. He had said, 'How will you survive in the wilderness? There are terrible creatures in the forest. We will have no home, nothing to eat except wild fruit. I cannot subject you to such hardship. I cannot take you with me, Sita.'

Sita had, for the first time in her life, spoken in a loud, defiant voice to Ram. 'I will not remain in the palace when you are living in the forest. I will go wherever you go. I would rather die than be without you. I shall walk in front of you on the forest path. I shall tread on the thorns and sharp stones to make them smooth for your feet. I implore you, my lord, do not leave me behind, for parting from you is crueler than death,' she had said and burst into tears. Ram had finally agreed to take her with him.

Sita recalled their beautiful hut in Chitrakoot, surrounded by trees and fragrant shrubs. Ram often pointed out the various flowering trees to her. He would pick up the flowers from the ground and show their colours to her. 'How beautiful the forest is. Listen to the birds singing, Sita. Can you hear how melodious and sweet their calls are?' he would say to her. They would sit outside their hut and watch the sky change colours at dawn. She had never known such peace and happiness before in her life.

'Will I ever touch your noble feet again to receive your blessings, or will I die without ever seeing you again?' Sita said to herself, covering her face with her hands as she wept.

That night she dreamt that Ram had sent her a message through a white swan.

'Beloved, if I were to die now and go to heaven, that heaven will be a void without you. My Sita, I have no existence without you. You are my soul, my vital breath. When I remember your gentle face but cannot see you, then this caressing breeze, so cool and fresh, burns me like fire. The sweet fragrance of flowers reminds me of you, but it only brings me pain.' Sita woke up and found her face was damp with tears.

Far away on a rocky hill, Ram sat with his brother Laxman, gazing beyond the vast sea. Hanuman had told him that Sita was a prisoner in the demon king Ravana's city of Lanka. His eyes were blurred with tears and his voice broke as he spoke to his brother. 'They say that if you lose someone dear to you, time will erase your grief. That is not true, Laxman. I cannot bear Sita's loss. My heart is torn by grief and it gets worse as time goes by. I feel so helpless. My Sita is suffering in a dark prison surrounded by demonesses. How she must have cried when Ravana seized her and carried her off. She must have called out my name. She must have cried over and over again but I was not there. O, Laxman, I have failed her. My heart burns with pain when I think of her suffering. Her agony is my agony too and when I think of my beloved Sita's anguish, it feels like every part of my body is pierced with needles.'

Laxman touched his brother's hand gently and said, 'Give up your grief and arm yourself with courage. Soon we shall destroy Ravana and rescue Sita. She will return to Ayodhya with you like the goddess of beauty and chastity that she is.'

War clouds, dark with fury and rage, gathered quickly. The deafening sounds of thunder could be heard as the gods in heaven came out to see the mighty battle about to begin. Ram's army swooped down on Lanka and the golden city began to burn as the war ravaged it. The fierce fighting between Ram's army of monkeys and bears and Ravana's demons raged on for weeks. Ravana's powerful army was defeated at last and the demon king was killed by Ram's mighty weapon—the Brahma Astra.

In the meantime, Sita sat alone in the grove, waiting for Ram to arrive. She had been told that he had won the battle and slayed Ravana. Somehow, she did not feel as overjoyed as she should have. A sliver of fear raced through her heart as she waited. A crow called incessantly in the garden. It was a bad omen and she knew in her heart that she would have to face some danger soon. Would she be killed by the demons before Ram could rescue her?

At last, Hanuman arrived. He bowed at her feet and said, 'My lord Ram says you are to be bathed and bedecked in jewels.'

'I would rather go as I am,' whispered Sita.

'You must obey my Lord Ram. Please bathe and adorn yourself. You will be carried in a palanquin through the city,' said Hanuman politely.

Accompanied by great confusion and noise, surrounded by crowds and shouts of joy, Sita's palanquin finally reached where Ram was seated. Sita began to tremble and could not lift her eyes to look at him. She cast her eyes down and bowed at his feet. 'Aaryaputra . . . I stand before you . . .' she said in a faint voice. Ram looked away and did not say anything for a few moments.

Then he spoke in a cold, indifferent tone she had never heard before. 'I have rescued you. I have done my duty as befits a king's honour but you cannot come with me. How can I take back a wife who has lived in a stranger's house for so long? You may go and live wherever you want. I cannot take you back to Ayodhya with me.'

Sita heard these harsh words without flinching though everyone around them stood frozen, stunned with shock. She looked up at Ram and said in a soft voice that all around them could not hear. 'These cruel words are not worthy of you, my lord. Have you forgotten that I am the daughter of Janaka, the great seer, and that he brought me up to be virtuous? Was it my fault that I was kidnapped and held prisoner? I have thought of no one but you during these dark days. But since you doubt my purity I will ask the god of fire, Agni, to take me. He knows my true self, even if you don't,' whispered Sita.

She then turned to Laxman and asked him to light a fire at once. Everyone waited for Ram to speak but he remained aloof, silently brooding. His face was impassive and he looked at Sita as if she were a stranger. Laxman reluctantly obeyed Sita and quickly built a huge fire.

'I bow before you, Agni. You, at least, know my purity, so take me as your own, 'she said and leapt into the flames. As everyone watched in horror the fire began to glow with a strange light and the flames rose high into the sky. The burning logs crackled and hissed as if a battle was raging within. The onlookers could not see Sita at all. She was totally engulfed by the flames.

Then suddenly a light flashed and the flames disappeared as the god of fire emerged, holding Sita in his arms. Bedecked in jewels and silken robes, she shone in all her glorious splendour. Ram gazed at her and said in a soft voice that only she could hear. 'Did you believe that I thought you were not as pure as the rivers in heaven? I had to do this to satisfy my people. What would they say if I had taken you without this fire purification? They would say I was blinded by love and had forgotten right from wrong.'

He reached his hand out and gently drew Sita to his side. As the heavens began to shower flowers upon them, he whispered in Sita's ears, 'Forgive me.' Sita smiled and bowed her head.

Together, they got into their flying chariot and headed back to Ayodhya. As they flew over the forest of Chitrakoot where they had lived so happily once, Sita looked down. Ram looked down too and Sita knew at once what was going through his mind. She saw the tears glisten on his face and all the sorrow of the last few cruel months was erased from her heart and her entire being was filled with love for her lord. Together they basked in the divine light that graced them from the gods in heaven, showering them with benevolence and bliss.

8

DRAUPADI & ARJUNA

Tragic Love

'Where are you going in the dead of the night?
To meet my lover who is life and death to me.
And are you not afraid to walk alone?
How can I be alone?
Love keeps me company.'

—Amaru, Amaru Shatakam

I am alone. Only the howling wind keeps me company. 'Arjuna, Arjuna'—I repeat his name to soothe my burning heart.

My eyes gleam with unshed tears as I remember my warrior husband, the love of my life. My heart is filled with a bittersweet pain and I know now that it means undying passion but stained with unrequited love. I had so little time with him. He was mine only once in four years and the year, so precious, flew away like a bird released from its cage. All I remember is how much I longed for him every minute and even when we were together, I could not be happy because I knew that soon he would leave me and I would be overwhelmed by this ache of being bereft once more.

I sit here, in the dying light, gazing upon the vast battlefield covered in blood. I see hundreds of men lying dead all around me but my heart feels no pain. I have forgotten how to feel anything; fear, love, passion and even my sense of innate pride, have all been erased from my being. That heady power of bittersweet revenge, now slowly seeps away too.

I only remember the faces of my five dead sons and I want to throw myself into the funeral pyres that burn all day on the battlefield but I know I have to wait for my death; I have to wait for the exact time the gods have decided for me to release my earthly body, even though I am only a walking corpse now. Like a shadow, I will live till that appointed time and I will try to remember who I once was; who was that proud, beautiful woman they called Draupadi? Shall I walk again through life with my love, with my Arjuna, the greatest warrior of our time, or shall I erase that heart-breaking memory forever and wait like an empty vessel for my life to end?

* * *

A fragrance of blue lotus blossoms rose from her body and spread in the air as she walked, mesmerizing all those who beheld her. Draupadi—a fire-born woman with eyes like a lotus, gleaming dark skin and midnight black hair that reached down to her ankles, was like a celestial maiden who, for some reason that only the gods knew, was born among men. Famed for her extraordinary sultry beauty, her fiery temperament and her innate pride, Draupadi was an unusual woman; a woman desired and coveted by any man who set eyes on her. They did not know that this was the woman who had been sent to bring about the destruction of an entire generation of Kshatriya men.

Draupadi was born from of a sacred fire during a 'yagna' organized by King Drupada. The king had longed for a child and had prayed for a long time to the gods to bless him with a son and heir. He wanted a son not just to carry on his name after him, to enable his soul to go to heaven when he died, but he wanted a son to take revenge on his arch enemy—Dronacharya.

King Drupada organized such a massive yagna that even the gods were impressed. From the sacred fire emerged a handsome, golden-skinned boy and when King Drupada saw him, he was filled with joy and happiness. 'At last, my wish has been granted. This son of mine will avenge me and restore my honour,' he said as he bowed his head to the gods. But when he reached his hand out to take the young boy, he heard a voice and stopped. 'We have another child for you, King Drupada,' the voice said. 'A girl.'

'A girl? I have no need for a girl. I only asked for a son, a valiant son who will defeat my enemy Dronacharya,' said Drupada, turning away. The voice fell silent but the flames of the yagna fire rose again, this time much higher. With a flash of golden light there appeared a girl. Tall and slender with polished dark skin and chiseled features, she stood proudly in the circle of blazing fire, gazing upon the world with luminous eyes that held a trace of haughty pride. All the kings and prices gathered at the yagna gasped with wonder as they beheld her. She was the most beautiful girl they had ever seen.

King Drupada hesitated and then reached forward to take her hand. 'I cannot refuse a gift from the heavens, so come with me, daughter. I shall call you Draupadi, after my own name,' he said, feeling a stab of remorse that he had not first accepted her with grace. He would have to take her; after all, she had been sent by the gods.

All her turbulent life; all through her endless trials, Draupadi could never forget those brief but traumatic moments when she stood before a father who had turned his face away from her. 'I will never bow before any man nor seek his approval as long as I live,' she often said to herself to calm the ache in her heart.

Her father King Drupada now treated her with great love and affection and allowed her to get her way in every matter. Unlike the other princesses at the court, she was allowed to ride horses, to learn how to use the weapons of warfare and even to sit next to the king when he held court. With her quick, sharp mind and the gift of speaking clearly and precisely, Draupadi soon became his favourite child.

King Drupada and his son Dhrishtadyumna both decided to hold a swayamvar' for Draupadi once she came of age. Princes were invited from all over the realm to a grand ceremony that was going to be held at the palace. This was going to be no ordinary swayamvar but one that even the gods in heaven were planning to watch with eager anticipation. Lord Krishna, a close friend and mentor to Draupadi, was going to be there too. In fact, it was he who had given her the name 'Krishnaa'.

Draupadi had heard the name Arjuna only once but it had created a strange, mysterious flutter in her heart. It was as if the name was etched in her mind; a name that belonged to her. Who was this Arjuna? Why was she longing to meet him? She was the princess of Panchala, she was the gorgeous Draupadi who could marry any man she wished to, yet the name Arjuna kept drumming in her head. Her heart, usually cold and indifferent to men, raced with excitement when she whispered this name. Why did she feel like this about a man she had never met? Was it because Krishna, her dearest friend, had mentioned him?

The sun seemed to shine even more brightly and the skies beamed down a brilliant golden light when she first set eyes on him. She knew at once he was a noble prince though he was dressed in the simple robes of a Brahmin. Bedecked in the finest silks and glittering with jewels, Draupadi sat at her swayamvar watching a line of noble princes trying to achieve success in a seemingly impossible task that had been set by her father and brother. Only the most skilled archer in the world would be able to send five arrows in succession through a revolving disc and hit the eye of a metal fish while looking at its reflection in a pool of water below. One by one all the noble princes tried and failed. Some could not even lift the bow and string the arrow, and they returned to their seats looking embarrassed and ashamed. Murmurs of protest could be heard now and many princes began to grumble that this task could not be achieved by any man, and that they had been invited to this gathering only to be insulted and humiliated by King Drupada.

Then rose a tall, handsome young man wearing golden armour, and as everyone watched, he picked up the bow effortlessly and took aim. 'He is Karna, the great archer, but he is the son of a charioteer. He was given a title along with the kingdom of Anga by Duryodhana so that he would fight on the side of the Kauravas forever.'

She saw the young man lift the bow and a wave of fear ran through Draupadi. She knew she had to stop him at once or all would be lost. 'Wait,' she cried out to the stunned assembly. 'Stop. You cannot take part in my swayamvar. You are a low--born man. I will not marry you even if you are able to hit the target. I will not be the wife of a man whose father is a charioteer and whose kingship has been acquired by charity,' she said, her eyes blazing with contempt.

Karna stood quietly for a few moments, staring at her, his face devoid of any expression, then he lifted the massive bow effortlessly and took aim. The entire assembly held their breath and the gods too looked away, though they knew what would happen. Karna shot his first arrow. It went flying through the air when a strange, trembling movement caused the arrow to turn suddenly and miss its target. A collective gasp of shock came from the crowd.

Karna, his face distorted with rage and humiliation, went back to his seat. Draupadi heaved a sigh of relief. She knew that Karna heard it because he turned and gave her a look of sheer hatred.

* * *

Was this the moment when all of Karna's anger and venom rose from Draupadi's rejection and from his public humiliation to form a knot in his heart? Was it this moment, when I insulted this warrior, who was said to be an equal to Arjuna, that I set in motion the wheels of my misfortune and sealed the cruel fate of thousands of other women who would become widows?

I now remember the voice that spoke to me at dawn on the day of my swayamvar. The sky was still grey with only a few streaks of silver-gold light. A bird began to sing but in a strange discordant tone, and then I heard a voice. It was so close to my ears that I thought I was dreaming but my eyes were wide open.

'Listen to me. I will not speak again to you till this cycle of your life on earth is over. Draupadi, listen to me carefully. You will marry five men, the greatest heroes of your time. You will be a queen and then a slave and then a queen again.

'You are gentle and kind, yet you will bring death to thousands of men. Thousands of women will become widows because of your desire for revenge.

'You will love with a true passion but you will not be loved in return by the man you love. You will only realize who truly loves you when it is too late.

'Lastly, in the hour of your death, you shall be alone.'

The voice fell silent as the sunlight streamed into my room. Was it a dream? In my pride and arrogance, I dismissed the prophesy. Arjuna. Where was Arjuna? That was my only thought.

* * *

Draupadi looked around the assembled crowd, at the dejected princes and kings. Then she looked at the man dressed in a Brahmin's simple robes. Who was he and what was he doing at her swayamvar? This event was only for royal Kshatriya men. He was tall and incredibly handsome, with a scar running down his arm. His dark, lotus eyes were bold and filled with a quiet confidence. He did not seem like a humble Brahmin. 'Who is this stranger?' Draupadi thought as she looked at him. Then she cast her eyes down. She must not seem too eager or the princes gathered in the assembly would get suspicious.

* * *

'He is Arjuna,' whispered Krishna's voice in my ears, though he was seated far away from me. Startled, I forgot to be modest and shy and stared boldly at the Brahmin now. Was this really Arjuna, the greatest archer of our time and my mentor Krishna's best friend? I knew he was the son of Kunti and later I came to know that he was the son of Indra, the king of heaven.

King Pandu could not father children. Kunti, his wife, had received a boon that enabled her to call upon the gods for a favour any time she wished. She asked the gods to give her sons. Yudhishthira was born of Dharma, Bheema of Vayu and Arjuna of Indra. Then Kunti helped Madri, King Pandu's second wife, to conceive Nakul and Sahadeva from the twin healer gods, the Ashvins. But I did not know all this at my swayamvar.

I also did not know that in my past life, impatient and impulsive as I am now, I had meditated on Lord Shiva. When the great lord appeared, I asked for a husband like him. He did not answer me for a few seconds so I asked him again and again. I asked him five times till he finally answered my prayer. He also said the qualities I had asked for in my husband could not be present in one, single mortal man. How did I know then that this episode from my past life would create so much heartbreak in my life as Draupadi? My five husbands would love and respect me but the one I loved the most would not return my love with an equal passion. Our hearts would entwine just briefly and then he would drift away from me.

But now, at this golden, auspicious hour of my swayamvara, Arjuna was before me and my heart was filled with joy.

* * *

As everyone watched, the Brahmin strung an arrow on the mighty bow with effortless grace and lifted it as if it were as light as a feather. A hushed silence fell over the assembly and even the birds stopped calling in the palace gardens. Then, with a quiet smile playing on his handsome face, the Brahmin took aim five times and hit the eye of the revolving fish with the arrow each time. For a few moments there was total silence and then an uproar broke out. The princes, shocked and furious with rage that a Brahmin had achieved this impossible task that the gathered Kshatriya princes had failed to do, now rose and began rattling their weapons angrily.

Draupadi ignored them and walked up to the man now standing before her, his dark eyes gleaming with admiration as he beheld her. Her heart flooded with love and her entire body trembled with a strange warmth she had never felt before as she placed the garland around his neck. She knew at once he was the chosen one; he was her destiny.

'Arjuna. Arjuna. I gift you Arjuna,' a voice whispered in her head and she turned to look at Lord Krishna. He was smiling at her gently, his beautiful eyes shining with happiness for them.

* * *

The assembly hall was filled with angry voices as pandemonium broke out. I don't know how we managed to get out. I shut my eyes and followed my husband. Later I was told that it was Bheema who held the princes off when they tried to attack us. By that time, I was married to all five brothers.

Why did Arjuna not protest? Why did he not say to his mother Kunti, 'This is Draupadi, my wife; she is only mine since I was the one who won her at the swayamvar and not my four brothers.' I often think about this as I sit by the battlefield. Whenever I complained to him about this unfair arrangement, this strange sharing of husbands, he would say, 'We have to obey our mother's word. I had no other choice.' I longed to be with him but the rule was that I should live with one brother for a year and no other brother could even look at me during that time.

My first year was spent with Yudhishthira, the eldest Pandava brother. He was a quiet, dignified and learned man but he was the one who would lose me later at a game of dice. My second husband was Bheema, a giant with a gentle and loving heart. He would do anything for me but I felt only a mild affection for him. I used him shamelessly because he was the only one who listened to my unending stream of vitriolic fury against the Kauravas and, later on, it was he who took a vow to take revenge on my behalf.

Then, finally, my year with Arjuna began. I was filled with ecstasy and I could not think of anything but my warrior husband, my true love. How swiftly that year flew! And how cruel time can be! With my other husbands, though they were kind and loving to me, time dragged its feet and each day seemed like an eternity. But when I was with Arjuna, day and night merged into one brief moment of sheer delight, only to vanish. One moment I was clasped in his battle-scarred arms and the next moment, I was alone in my bed, my skin still warm from his caresses.

I tried my very best to keep him with me, using all my womanly skills of seduction.

Every night during my year with Arjuna, I bathed myself in rose water, braided jasmine flowers in my hair and waited for him to come to me. How I longed for him, my heart heavy with a sweet sorrow as I watched the night fade away. Some nights he would suddenly appear at my door and then I felt my bedchamber itself enclosed heaven. Stars danced around me and the moon descended on my bed as I beheld his handsome face. My longing for my husband melted away as we embraced and I would be completely lost in a vast, blissful world where nothing else existed but Arjuna and I. Soon, very soon, he would gently pull himself away from my arms. I would cling to him, beg him to stay for a few more precious moments. 'Panchali, my beloved. I cannot tear myself away from you but I have so many duties to perform,' he always said, holding me as if he would not let me go. Yet, he was forever leaving me to travel to the distant mountains. 'Why do you go away from me and erode our brief moments of love? Our time together is too fleeting as it is. We only have a year together and then I have to wait for another four years for you to come to me,' I would lament, but he never replied.

Only once had I caught a flash of jealousy in his eyes and then it vanished. I think he could not bear the thought of my being with his brothers and that is why he escaped to the high mountains, to meditate on Lord Shiva or to fight some battle.

While I waited for Arjuna, I cherished the memory of our time together, guarded each moment like a thief guards his stolen jewels. I often thought of the day Arjuna brought me a rare flower; the day he bathed my forehead with a dew-drenched leaf when we were roaming the forest. I, who had never seen dust on my feet, now walked on rocky, muddy paths with my five husbands. Their evil cousins the Kauravas had fixed for them to be banished yet again. Bheema once offered to carry me but Kunti would not allow it since it would create disharmony amongst the brothers.

A few years went by and I began to wonder if Arjuna really loved me. Was I just a prize he had won; a prize that acclaimed him as the greatest archer of our time? I was shattered when I heard that he had married Krishna's sister Subhadra. How could he do this to me? Was I, Draupadi, the most beautiful woman on earth, not enough for him? He brought her to meet me and when I saw the love in his eyes for this innocent, beautiful girl, I was filled with a jealousy so powerful that I could have killed that young girl with my bare hands if she had not been Krishna's sister. I saw Kunti watching me. I knew she could read my mind because she told Subhadra to come away. Arjuna followed her, holding her hand, giving her tender looks. He had never looked at me like that.

A year later he took two more wives, Ulupi and Chitrangada. I told myself that I could not expect him to be celibate while he waited for his year with me; I consoled myself that I meant more to him than any other woman.

Once, overcome with jealousy, I accused Krishna of plotting against me. 'Why did you get him to marry your sister? I thought you were my friend.'

He gave me an amused look and said, 'Krishnaa, always remember that Arjuna is never going to be tied to you. He comes and goes of his own free will. You know that his commitment to you is true, so calm your jealousy. It was predestined that he should marry Subhadra and from their union will be born Abhimanyu—a great warrior.'

His words did nothing to soothe me. I knew now that I was born to be unhappy; I was born to create strife amongst men. A few golden moments of happiness did come my way and I held on to them tightly, like a drowning man clutches a rope thrown to save him. I caressed my body and thought of Arjuna's hands caressing me. I shut my eyes and touched my lips, compelling myself to believe it was Arjuna whose lips were touching mine.

'Panchali'—that was Arjun's name for me. I often heard him whispering my name though we were careful never to look at each other when I was with one of his brothers. I knew that a deep-rooted anger and resentment festered in his heart about the way our lives had turned out but he kept it well hidden. I could sense it even though he rarely looked into my eyes; rarely revealed his heart to me.

Then came the year that changed our lives forever. Yudhishthira was invited to a game of dice by Duryodhana, the eldest Kaurava. Aided by his wily uncle Shakuni, who was an expert at cheating at gambling, my noble husband lost everything—his kingdom, his wealth and his brothers.

He lost me too. I was now a slave to the Kauravas.

Duryodhana, who had coveted me for a long time, was thrilled to have me as his slave. Now helped by his brother, Dushasana, he tried to disrobe me in front of an entire assembly of men; each man watched me being shamed and did nothing to help. These were all men of noble birth yet no one came to my rescue. I was called vile names and jeered at.

'Come and sit on my lap, gorgeous Draupadi, who likes being the wife of several men,' laughed Dushasana, patting his thighs. My five husbands sat looking dazed. They were now slaves and could do nothing. 'Help me, Arjuna,' I cried but he turned his face away. Bheema was the only one who tried to come to my rescue but the Kauravas began to shout. 'Leave her. She belongs to us now.'

Bheema gave a roar of despair as he let go of me, his face distraught with anger and helplessness. 'I will break Dushasana's legs one day. I will drink the blood from Duryodhana's heart. I will avenge this dishonour you are facing today. I promise you,' he whispered.

Duryodhana now began pulling at my saree and I knew there was only one person in this world I could ask for help. I closed my eyes and began to call Krishna's name over and over again. He did not appear. I was trembling with shame and fear but in my heart a rage began to burn; this was the rage, this was the fire that would burn all the Kauravas.

Duryodhana kept pulling my saree but the garment stretched on endlessly. Yards of cloth now unravelled as he pulled and pulled, yet I was still fully clothed. Finally, Duryodhana fell on the floor exhausted and I knew who had saved me.

I began walking away but then I stopped and turned my face to the Kauravas.

I gathered all my strength and I cursed them.

'Listen to me, you evil men who possess no Kshatriya honour. I, Draupadi, curse you all. Your entire clan will be annihilated and there will be not one son left in your family to burn your funeral pyres.' My voice echoed through the huge hall and everyone fell silent. I knew then that I had been was born from the yagna fire for this day. I knew now why I was also called Yagnaseni.

Our years of exile began. Arjuna, my husband, who once looked at me with liquid eyes filled with passion, now wore a hard, cold look on his face. He refused to meet my eyes though I had forgiven him for not saving me when I was being disrobed by Duryodhana. Bheema still muttered under his breath about avenging my honour. 'I will not tie my hair till I wash my hair with the blood from Duryodhana's heart,' I said to him, as the desire for revenge became the core of my being.

I tried not to think of how Arjuna had failed me. 'I love you with all my being. I know you would have helped me if you had been a free man,' I said to him one day as we walked in the forest.

'How can I call myself your husband when I could do nothing to help you? I am too ashamed to even touch a strand of your hair. I do not deserve you, my precious Panchali,' he said, and for the first time I saw tears in my warrior husband's eyes. I knew then that he loved me more than his other wives. I meant more to him than any other women on this earth but somehow it did not soothe my jealous, greedy heart. I wanted so much more from him. I wanted him to be a part of my entire being and not a lover to be shared with other women.

This was our last year together though I did not know it. The thunderclouds of the war that would kills thousands of men were looming on the horizon but I, obsessed with Arjuna and the desire for revenge, could not see them.

I did wash my hair with Duryodhana's blood; I did laugh with glee when I heard that Bheema had broken Dushasana's thighs, but as the killing went on, the fire of revenge began to die in my heart.

It was too late.

Now I sit here all alone. Soon we will begin our final journey to the high mountains. Arjuna's hands touched mine briefly for one last time and then he went away to mourn his son Abhimanyu's death.

* * *

As she and the five Pandavas walked, Draupadi was the first one to fall. 'I must go and help her,' cried Bheema.

'Leave her. It was her destiny to fall first. She always loved Arjuna more that any one of us so she must pay for that sin,' said Yudhishthira, not stopping to look back. Arjuna heard him and continued to gaze up towards the mountains. His beloved Panchali had fallen down lifeless a few steps behind him but he did not turn around. He could see in his mind's eye, his proud, beautiful Panchali lying dead on the ground. The pain in his heart was unbearable but he consoled himself with the thought that he would meet her in heaven.

As Arjuna walked ahead to meet his own death, he prayed to the gods; he prayed to Krishna, his saviour and Draupadi's beloved friend and protector, that they would be united again in heaven. Their fragmented and fragile love would be entire and whole during their next life. Draupadi would belong to him.

'She will be mine and mine alone,' he whispered as he gave up his life.

9

GANGA & SHANTANU

An Unquestioning Love

'Dearest heart, if you will love me true,
What use are joys of heaven to me?
But if you will not love me true,
What use are joys of heaven to me?'

—Shudraka, Mrichchhakatika

The sun, a magnificent golden orb of fire, was setting on the horizon, casting a rosy glow on the shimmering waters of the river Ganga. The trees beyond the river were slowly turning into dark silhouettes and the birds, roosting on their branches, sang a few soft notes, as if bidding a gentle farewell to the setting sun.

King Shantanu, the handsome young ruler of Hastinapur, walked along the banks of the swiftly flowing river, admiring the beautiful sunset. He had just finished hunting and now, tired and weary from the endless chase over the hills and ravines to catch his prey, he wanted to enjoy the cool breeze along the riverside. He stopped and dipped his hands into the flowing river and sprinkled a few drops of the ice-cold water on his face, offering a silent prayer to the golden sun about to disappear over the horizon. Then, as he lifted his face, he was astounded by an extraordinary vision that appeared suddenly before him.

A tall, graceful woman, dressed in a white gossamer saree and wearing a garland of rare blue lotus blossoms around her neck, stood before him. A strange, soft light danced around her and lit up her exquisitely beautiful face as she smiled at him. The young king had never seen such a stunning woman in his entire life. Many noble princesses of great beauty had been presented to him as his future brides but none of them had the effect of the woman standing in front of him.

As the sky turned from gold to silver, King Shantanu stood silently, unable to move or speak. His mind was in turmoil; he could not breathe properly but he knew for certain that for the first time in his life he had fallen in love. This beautiful woman who had appeared before him out of nowhere had changed his life in just a few fleeting moments, and as the last rays of the sunlight left the earth, he knew he could not live without her; he knew that he had to marry her and be with her forever.

He walked up to her and said, 'I am the king of Hastinapur. Tell me your name, fair maiden.'

She lifted her beautiful eyes, which shone with a strange light, and smiled at him. Shantanu felt his heart beating like a drum in his chest and he could hardly speak. He hesitated for a few moments to catch his breath. 'O gentle maiden! Will you marry me and be my queen?' he asked in a quiet, tremulous voice. He had never felt so weak and helpless before in his life. He was King Shantanu, a great warrior, famed all over the kingdom for his valour; he was the bravest of the brave, a royal being, descended from an ancient, noble family of kings, yet he could hardly utter these few words without his voice trembling. He felt as if he had been struck by a bolt of lightning and would never be able to move again.

The woman smiled, her beautiful eyes sparkling, but remained silent. Her face seemed to glow with a mysterious, inner light as the last faint rays of sunlight caressed her. Her tall, graceful body seem to float in the air. 'Who was this woman? Where had she suddenly appeared from?' he thought. The king, beginning to feel nervous and agitated now, asked her again, forcing himself to speak in a louder voice this time. He could not bear the thought of this beauty refusing him. 'What if she goes away and I never see her again? What if she is offended by my proposal and refuses me?' he thought, his heart sinking rapidly with dread. He knew he would die if she did not accept his proposal.

The sky was an inky blue now and the shadows of the trees swayed on the banks of the river. The birds had fallen silent and King Shantanu felt that the entire world was standing still. Even the river seemed to have stopped flowing. 'Please, dear gods in heaven. If I have ever done any good deeds then please make her accept me,' he prayed silently as he waited for the woman to speak.

After a few excruciatingly long moments, which seemed like a lifetime to the king, the woman spoke in a soft, melodious voice.

'O noble king of Hastinapur. I am Ganga and I will become your wife but only if you agree to my conditions,' she said.

The king, overjoyed and thrilled to hear her speak these words, readily agreed. He was bewildered by his intense passion for this stranger yet he had never known such happiness. This rare beauty had agreed to be his wife. He was the luckiest man on earth.

'Whatever you say, my love, I will do. I will give you my entire kingdom. I will give you my life,' he said, his voice breaking with happiness.

'I do not want your kingdom or your life, noble king. I only ask these few things of you. Listen to me very carefully. The first is that you will never question what I do, however strange or irrational it may seem to you. The second is that you will never prevent me from doing what I desire. If you ever stop me from doing whatever task I am doing, and if you ever break these promises, I shall leave you,' she said quietly.

The king was slightly surprised at this strange request but he was so enamoured by this gorgeous woman, so blindly in love with her, that he did not want to think too much about what she had said. This exquisite beauty had agreed to become his wife and that was all that mattered to him. He could not ask for anything more.

'I agree to whatever you ask. Just promise to be my wife and live with me forever. Be my queen,' he said, bowing his head to a woman for the first time in his life.

'I, Ganga, accept your proposal to be your wife, noble king,' said the woman, reaching her hand out to him and his heart filled with incredible joy as she touched him.

They were soon married and everyone in the kingdom was amazed to see how much their king adored his queen. 'She seems to have bewitched him. But she is a noble, good lady so all should be well for them. May she bring him happiness and joy forever,' they said.

A year later, a son was born to them but before the king could celebrate the birth of his first-born prince, his wife took the baby to the river and drowned him. The king was shocked and horrified but he remained silent since he had given her his promise to never question what she did. His heart was filled with sorrow at the loss of his son, but he loved his queen so much that he was helpless to do anything. He decided to ignore this horrible incident and hoped they would have more sons. Though she had shocked and hurt him with this terrible act, King Shantanu still loved his Ganga as intensely as he had done when he first saw her.

'I will continue to love her whatever happens. She is the reason I live and she can do whatever she wants. A man can love a woman in so many different ways. If my love wants me to never question her, I shall do so. All I want is for us to be together forever. She is a gift to me from heaven,' thought the king, gazing at his wife with adoration.

'She had made these conditions before we were married and I must abide by them. I will never question her. I will let her do anything she wants even if it shocks and upsets me. All I ask is that she stays with me and never stops loving me. My love for her is unconditional and unwavering. I will love her till I die.'

As the years passed, King Shantanu watched in total silence and bewilderment as his wife gave birth to six more sons and drowned each of their newborn babies in the river. As the king stood frozen with horror and shock, she picked up each infant boy as soon as he was born, carried him swiftly to the river and threw him into the flowing waters. She came home looking very pleased with herself, as if she had not done such a cruel deed. King Shantanu was now distraught with grief but he still remained silent. His love for his wife did not lessen but he had to use all his willpower to remain silent and not question her. At night he gazed at her beautiful face and could not help wondering where she had come from. She did not seem like an ordinary woman. 'No ordinary woman would ever harm her own flesh and blood,' he thought, saddened by her behaviour. Yet King Shantanu continued to love his Ganga.

He stood by quietly, watching his wife kill each of their seven sons. But when the eighth baby was born, the king could no longer restrain himself. 'Stop. Why are you doing such a terrible thing? Have you no love for our newborn sons? What kind of a mother does such a cruel act? You have killed all my sons but I will not let you drown this one. I have loved you with all my heart but I will not let you take my son away. Do not be so heartless and cruel,' he shouted, his shock and his grief making him forget his promise to her.

Ganga stood holding the baby in her arms. She looked at King Shantanu with sadness in her lovely eyes and then spoke in a quiet voice. 'O king, you have broken your promise to me. I will have to leave you now but listen to me before you judge me,' she said. 'I am Ganga, a celestial being, and I live in heaven. One day, eight vasus, celestial beings like me, came to me with a request. These eight vasus had committed the terrible sin of stealing Sage Vasistha's sacred cow and had been cursed by the sage to go down to the earth and live as mortal beings. Distraught and frightened by this curse, the eight vasus requested my help to shorten their lives on earth. "O Ganga. Please become our mother on earth and release us from this curse. Let us be born to you as humans and then kill us at once so that we don't have to spend any time on earth," they begged. So I changed my form to that of a human maiden and married you. I have given birth to seven vasus and then drowned them at once in the river to send them back to heaven immediately. You saw me doing this and yet you did not ask me why. Now since you have broken your promise, I must leave you and return to heaven. I will take this eighth son of ours with me but I promise to return him to you. He has to live his entire life on earth. You shall earn your merit later in heaven.'

As soon as King Shantanu heard this, he fell at Ganga's feet. 'I beg your forgiveness. Please do not leave me. Stay here on earth and bring up this son of ours. I should have realized as soon as I saw you on the banks of the river so many years ago, that you were a celestial being. No mortal woman could be so beautiful as you, my love. Please do not go away. I will never question you again. I will allow you to do whatever you wish,' said the king, tears running down his face.

Ganga shook her head. She put her hand out and gently touched the king's face to wipe his tears away. 'I have to leave. My time on earth has ended. I have been very happy with you since you have loved me so truly, but now I must return to heaven. I will bring up our son in the best possible way and return him to you soon. I shower you with my blessings,' she said and before Shantanu could say anything more, she disappeared into the sky, carrying the baby in her arms.

King Shantanu stood still, watching her as she slowly merged into the clouds. Distraught with grief, he lifted his face to the sky and cried, 'I want to end my life right now. My heart is shattered into a thousand pieces yet I must go on living. She has promised to return our son to me. I shall live in hope of that joyous day. I will cherish her memory forever. I only wish I had known that she was no ordinary woman but a goddess. I wish I had learnt to worship her. I regret that I treated her like a human being; I regret I questioned what she did. I should have loved her silently and always allowed her to do as she wished. O Ganga! When will I see you again?' sobbed the king, still gazing up at the empty sky, his heart heavy with sorrow.

From that day onward, the king retreated into a quiet corner of his palace, a sad and broken man. He lived as an ascetic, carrying out his duties as king, but the deep sadness never left him. He waited for the day his son would be returned to him and he could live again. He walked to the river every day, his eyes eagerly scanning the horizon for any sign of his beloved Ganga and his son, but each day he returned to the palace disappointed. The people of the kingdom were bewildered by their king's intense sorrow and wondered where their beautiful queen had gone.

King Shantanu spoke to no one about his grief and quietly retreated more and more into himself. At night he gazed at the sky and wondered if Ganga was there amongst the stars with other celestial beings. 'Does she remember our life together or has she forgotten this ordinary mortal begin who was once her husband; who loved her more than his life?' Sometimes while walking along the river, Shantanu would imagine Ganga floating towards him and he would cry out in joy but then he would realize it was only the mist shimmering in a strange way and his heart would be filled with sadness and loss again.

Just when he was giving up all hope of ever seeing his son, one day, the king caught a glimpse of a sudden movement on the river Ganga from the palace windows. He ran out at once, his feet bare, his head uncovered, shocking the guards and the courtiers. 'Has the king lost his senses?' they asked each other.

King Shantanu arrived at the riverbank, breathless, his heart racing with nervous anticipation. He knew something was about to happen, something great and wonderful, yet his mind was filled with fear. How he had waited for this day, praying that Ganga would keep her promise to him. 'What if she forgot all about him when she returned to heaven?' he thought, darts of fear piercing his entire being. Suddenly, a huge wave rose in the water and the goddess appeared in all her splendid glory. She was dressed in pristine white and bedecked with jewels. Golden rays shimmered all around her as she stood in the river holding a child in her arms. She smiled at King Shantanu and said, 'You thought I had forgotten all about my promise to you? Here is your son; here is the eighth son I bore you. His name is Devavrata. He has been brought up by me in heaven. He has learnt the art of warfare, he has mastered the Vedas and is skillful in statecraft already, though he is only a child. Take him with you, bring him up now with great care and know that in the future he will be the greatest hero the world will ever know.' Saying this, she handed the child to King Shantanu. The king was about to speak to her, to tell her how much he still loved and longed for her but the clouds descended and she disappeared.

King Shantanu knew he would never see her again as long as he lived on earth. He picked up his son in his arms and held him tightly. The boy looked up at him and smiled. For a brief moment, he looked so much like Ganga that Shantanu's heart leapt with joy. Then he remembered that she had gone forever. His son, so beautiful and bathed with a heavenly glow, was now his only link to his lost love; his goddess who had lived with him on earth; his Ganga whom he had loved with all his heart.

This young boy, the son of Ganga and King Shantanu, would grow up to become the greatest warrior of his time and one day he would take a vow of celibacy and be known from then on, as Bhishma.

Years later, King Shantanu would marry another, but he never forgot his heavenly love and every time he would see his son, he would feel consoled by the thought that this was his beloved wife Ganga's son. 'I hope and pray that one day Ganga and I shall be together again,' he said to soothe his aching heart, while the river flowed and sparkled far away, carrying the weight of his words.

Often at night, her would hear his beloved Ganga's voice, singing to him softly from beyond the clouds, filling his heart with joy.

10

RUKMINI & KRISHNA

Love and Victory

'O dearest one!
If thou extinguish not the fire of desire
Kindled by the melodious music of thy flute,
By thy sidelong glances,
By thy bewitching smiles,
Then my body will be burnt by this fire
As well as by separation from thee,
O dearest heart, let me attain thy nearness
By meditating on thy feet.'

—Bhagavata Purana

The gentle blue of a cloudless sky, the deep azure of the ocean and the shimmering, mysterious blue of a peacock's feather; Rukmini shut her eyes and thought about all the colours that shone on Krishna's beautiful face. She had never seen the blue god, yet his glorious image loomed in front of her eyes constantly. She knew what he looked like from a previous life, and she held this image secretly in her heart, cherishing it and loving it.

She knew he was the chosen one for her. Every heartbeat, every breath of hers belonged only to him. She felt that she had been born on this earth only to belong to him. From the time she was a young girl, Rukmini had made up her mind that she would be Krishna's bride one day.

Her father, the king of Vidarbha, knew about her deep, constant love for Krishna and he and his queen were keen she should wed him when she came of age. 'There is no better bridegroom for my beautiful daughter. She will be so fortunate to be his wife. She will lead a life of eternal bliss by his side. She will be blessed by the gods,' he said to his wife. They wished with all their hearts that this match would happen one day but there was a huge obstacle to their desire. Their son Rukmi hated Krishna with a passion.

'He killed Kansa, our kinsman. How can my sister be married to him? We can never allow such an alliance,' he raged. 'What will Jarasandha, the emperor of Magadha, say? Have you thought of that, father? Krishna has slayed his son-in-law and widowed both his daughters. We owe allegiance to the emperor. Don't forget that. Krishna is Jarasandha's enemy and thus he is our enemy too. We cannot afford to displease our mighty emperor. Forget about marrying our Rukmini to Krishna.'

The old king of Vidarbha nodded his head timidly. He was afraid of his son's wrath and decided not to mention Krishna's name again. He secretly hoped that his daughter Rukmini would marry Krishna but he did not know how this would happen. His son was already preparing to go to war against Krishna, along with the other allies of Emperor Jarasandha, to take revenge for the death of Kansa, the late king of Mathura.

Rukmi had other plans too. He had promised Shishupala, the prince of Chedi and a favourite of the emperor, that Rukmini would be married to him. 'This way we can please Emperor Jarasandha too. He will bestow many gifts upon Shishupala, and Rukmini will become the wealthiest woman in our realm. It will be a perfect match and we will all benefit from it,' he said gleefully.

Rukmini was aghast when she heard about this. 'How dare my brother trade me like this to please his allies? I will never marry that evil Prince Shishupala. I would rather die,' she cried.

When she confronted Rukmi, he admonished her. 'You will do as your father and I say. Forget about that cowherd claiming to be a royal. You will be married to Shishupala in three days,' said Rukmi.

Rukmini, alone in her grief and anger, fled to the palace garden. She hid herself within a grove of trees and thought for a long time. 'What should I do? There is no one here who can help me. My brother hates Lord Krishna with a passion and my father will not go against my brother. I cannot marry that evil Shishupala. I must seek help to escape from this dreadful match and marry Lord Krishna, my true beloved. Whom can I can turn to? Who will rescue me? I can only hope and pray that the gods in heaven will help me and I will become Krishna's bride. Please, please send me some hope; some sign that my wish will come true,' she said, gazing up at the sky, her lovely face pale and worried.

Suddenly, a cool breeze touched her face and a shower of blossoms began to cascade down slowly on her head. It was as if an invisible being was blessing her; soothing her troubled, aching heart. Rukmini looked up as a streak of silver light flashed in the sky. She hurriedly rose to her feet. The sky was sending out waves of shimmering blue light that circled around her, bathing her entire body with a warm iridescent light.

Blue. Blue. Blue. The entire world had turned blue. Rukmini let herself be engulfed by the blue waves of this blissful sea of light. She was no longer worried or sad; a feeling of immense joy raced through her heart. 'I know what I will do. I will ask Krishna to help me,' she thought. Then she laughed with delight and said the words aloud to herself. 'I will write a letter to him and ask him to come and take me away. He, a man of noble birth, has a right to carry away the bride of his choice, especially when the bride is imploring him to do so.'

Once Rukmini had made up her mind she felt like a new person. She spoke to no one about her plan. She did not want her brother to hear of it. He would lock her up for sure and force her to marry Shishupala. 'He wants to sell me to please the emperor. I will never let it happen,' she said.

Rukmini waited impatiently for her parents and the maids in the palace to fall asleep and then she lit a lamp and stole away to a small hidden room in a corner of the palace. She sat down and began to write. At first, she could not think of the right words, but then the pen slowly began to write as if by itself.

Her lifelong devotion to Krishna, her innermost desires and her absolute love for him flowed on to the paper. She had to stop herself from writing as page after page filled the room. All the unspoken thoughts that had remained quietly hidden in her heart now burst forth like a spring emerging from the earth. There was so much to say to her beloved. But she forced herself to put the pen down. 'No. I should not write him such a long letter. I will just beg him to come and take me away; take his rightful bride away. I know there will be a battle but I am not afraid. Nothing more needs to be said. Krishna will know what is in my heart.'

Early the next morning, when the palace was still asleep, Rukmini called a priest who had always been her trusted advisor and guide. 'Please, take this letter to Dwarka.' The old Brahmin nodded. He did not ask her who the letter was meant for. He had always known that Krishna was the only one for Rukmini and knew that Krishna was the intended recipient. He took the letter from her and quickly went out of the palace. As he hurried towards Dwarka, he prayed that Rukmini's wishes would come true.

Krishna received the letter and smiled as he read it. Then he spoke to his brother Balaram. 'She asks me to come and take her away. How brave she is. She says she is not afraid of the battle that will certainly follow. Does she not know how keen I am to marry her? I had sent a proposal to her father but that coward brother of hers rejected it.'

Balaram looked at Krishna, his eyes brimming with love and affection, and then reached out and clasped his brother's hand. 'We will go right now, my brother, to get your bride for you. She is the chosen one for you. She is the queen that Dwarka needs. She is Goddess Laxmi incarnate. Your bride waits. Let us not waste time. We shall go fetch her even if we have to go into battle.'

* * *

The streets of Kundina, the capital of Vidarbha, were decorated with flowers; its citizens had filled the streets with hundreds of earthernware pots of incense to perfume the air. Rukmini woke up at dawn and watched the sky change colour. Soon the blue god would be with her. She waited for her maids to come and get her ready. She sat quietly as they bathed and dressed her in the finest of silks. They put fresh flowers in her hair and painted her feet with red alta. They adorned her with gold and diamond jewellery. When Rukmini had finished getting ready and came out of her room, the entire palace was stunned by her beauty. 'It seems Goddess Laxmi herself has come to down to earth,' they whispered as she walked past them.

Rukmini did not hear or see anyone. She felt as though she were walking in a dream. All the while the maids had been dressing her in silks and bedecking her with jewels, she had been thinking of Krishna.

Soon he would be here. She would finally set eyes on her beloved lord. She did not worry about the mayhem that would ensue once her brother saw that Krishna had come to take her away.

At that moment, Rukmi was strutting around the palace proudly, feeling very pleased with himself since he believed his sister was going to marry Shishupala today. 'With the emperor's favourite as my brother-in-law I will become really powerful and everyone will treat me with awe and respect,' he thought as he watched the wedding preparations. He was surprised that his headstrong, willful sister had agreed so meekly to this match.

All their allies knew that Krishna had asked for Rukmini's hand but he had been rejected. Jarasandha was extremely pleased that the family had chosen Shishupala instead. What a slap in that Yadav cowherd's face! Rukmi could never forget how many times he had been badly thrashed by Krishna in battle. His wore his humiliation and shameful defeat like battle scars on his body. Today he would walk victorious and proud knowing he had a hand in turning the cowherd into a sad, rejected suitor. Rukmi stroked his moustache and laughed. As he stepped out of the palace, he saw a beautifully decorated golden palki slowly moving towards the palace gates.

'Where is the princess going to now?' he asked, a worried frown on his face.

'To the temple of Gauri, O prince. Every new bride goes to this temple to seek Goddess Parvati's blessings before the wedding ceremony,' said a minister, bowing. 'Look, the people of the entire city have come out on the streets to greet the Princess Rukmini before her wedding.'

Rukmi narrowed his eyes and watched the palki as it was carried slowly through the crowds. People were calling out

Rukmini's name and scattering rose petals on the path of the palki. There was not an inch of space to be seen on the street that led to the temple.

Rukmi frowned. For some reason he felt uneasy about the crowd. He heard someone shout Krishna's name. Why would they do that? The cowherd was nowhere around even though his father had invited him to the wedding despite Rukmi's protests. 'He is the king of Dwarka. We must invite all the noble princes. It is the correct way,' his father had said.

Rukmi turned to the minister. 'Make sure there are guards near the princess all the time. I don't want any trouble from the crowds,' he said.

When the palki reached the temple, Rukmini alighted and cast her eyes down as she walked up the temple steps slowly and gracefully. Her heart was racing. She was worried that Krishna might be stopped from coming to the temple. She folded her palms and whispered, 'Maa Gauri, I have come to seek your blessings. I beg you to give me the husband of my choice. You married Lord Shiva against your father's wishes. My father is for my marriage to Krishna but my brother wants me to marry another. Help me. O Devi! Consort of Lord Shiva. Let the blue god carry me away, I pray to you. Please let Krishna and only Krishna wed me.'

The princess washed the goddess's feet and placed an offering of fruit and flowers before her. Then she sat down and spent a long time praying as the crowd waited patiently outside, wanting to catch yet another glimpse of their beautiful princess.

When she came out and began walking down the temple steps, surrounded by a flank of palace guards, she heard someone shout out Krishna's name. She lifted her face in surprise and her heart leapt with joy. 'He will come soon. He will be here soon,' she said to herself as she looked around anxiously. A sea of faces stood like a wall before her. Among them were the kings of neighbouring states, princes from far-off lands, palace guards and thousands of ordinary people. Where was Krishna? Where was the dark one with a peacock feather in his crown? She knew he wore yellow robes. But she could not see anyone in the crowd who looked like Krishna. Though she had never seen him, she knew she would recognize him at once because his image was carved in her heart. Why could she not find him? Where was her beloved? Had he not come to get her? A sense of deep despair now flooded over her and she began to feel dizzy.

Out of nowhere, a blinding light streaked over her head and she heard thunder in the sky. Though it was bright daylight, a circle of dark clouds formed a canopy over her and the light changed from gold to dark blue. It was as if the heavens had sent a curtain of mist and clouds to hide her. Suddenly someone took her hand and she heard a soft voice whisper, 'Rukmini, my beloved.' She laughed out in delight. He was here. He was standing next to her. She lifted her eyes to look upon his beautiful dark face. Then she quickly cast them down again; his gorgeous, shimmering aura was far too powerful for her to bear.

'Come, let us go,' he said, and together they stepped into his chariot. Rukmini clung to his arm, afraid that someone would snatch her away from Krishna. She could hear people shouting but she could not make out if they were angry or delighted that Krishna was taking her away. He was taking what rightfully belonged to him. Her brother and Shishupala would now fly into a furious rage. They would try and stop them somehow. Rukmini told herself to stay calm. She was with her beloved Krishna and that was all that mattered to her.

As soon as the wheels of the chariot began to move, raising a blinding flurry of dust, chaos erupted all around them.

'Stop! Stop them!' someone shouted but the onlookers were too stunned to do anything.

Krishna laughed as he sped away in his chariot carrying Rukmini, his bride-to-be. He heard his old enemy Jarasandha's voice screaming in rage, 'You fools! Why are you all just standing around, doing nothing? Go after them. He cannot get away. Stop him.'

Shishupala, Rukmi and the other princes, who were standing frozen in shock, were now rudely jolted into action. They quickly ordered their armies to give chase. Krishna turned around and said to Rukmini. 'Can you handle the chariot while I deal with these hoards chasing us?' Rukmini nodded. He did not know how well she could handle horses and effortlessly control a speeding chariot. She was pleased that he had asked her; that he had faith in her ability to handle the chariot.

Rukmini grasped the reins expertly and held the speeding chariot steady while Krishna shot arrows at lightning speed at the pursuing enemies. Rukmini saw that Krishna was covered with dust and so was she. Then Krishna pointed to a whirlpool of dust far way. 'Look. There is my brother Balaram. He will take care of the enemy now. They don't know that a hurricane is coming towards them; a hurricane that will flatten them out!' he said and laughed.

Rukmini held the reins firmly as the horses raced through the narrow, muddy lanes and Krishna looked at her and smiled. Without saying a word, they both knew that they belonged to each other and had loved each other with a true passion for many lives. Rukmini's entire body was overwhelmed with such an intense feeling of love that she began to tremble. She wanted to throw her arms around him but she had to keep her hands on the reins of the speeding chariot. As if reading her mind, the blue god whispered, 'We shall be together eternally, my love. You shall soon be my queen.'

Suddenly, they heard a shout. Her brother Rukmi appeared right behind them. 'You cowherd. I will break every bone in your body. Today, I will crush you. You have dared to insult me and my clan by abducting my sister,' he yelled, his voice shaking with rage as he tried to crash his chariot into theirs.

Rukmini wanted to shout back at her brother but Krishna held up his hand to silence her. 'Keep the chariot steady,' he said. He watched quietly as Rukmi's chariot came closer and closer to them. Then, in one swift move, he let fly a single, diamond-tipped arrow. It flew with blinding speed and hit Rukmi's chariot, shattering it into pieces. Rukmi fell to the ground with a loud cry. He quickly started crawling behind the broken wheels to hide. Then he took up his sword, but Krishna sent another arrow at him, slicing his sword into half. Rukmi now lay helplessly on the ground and Krishna, having dismounted the chariot and advanced towards Rukmi, raised his sword over his head.

'O, spare my brother's life. Let him go, my lord,' Rukmini cried, though she herself was furious at her brother. But she could not let him die. She did not want Krishna's hands to be stained with her brother's blood.

'Let him go,' she cried again.

Krishna held his sword high over Rukmi's bowed head and as Rukmini screamed, he brought the sharp edge down on his head. Rukmini shut her eyes and began to sob. Then she heard Krishna laugh. She opened her eyes, fear shaking her entire body, and saw that her brother was still alive.

'Look, my beloved. Your brother lives. All I have done is shave a bit of hair from his arrogant head and cut off half of his haughty moustache. Let his allies see him in this new form now,' said Krishna, clapping his hands and roaring with laughter.

Balaram's chariot now appeared. He got down and, after bowing to Rukmini, he went and stood near Krishna. He touched his shoulder gently and whispered a few words to him. 'Let him go, brother. Why humiliate him in this cruel manner? He is our kinsman, do not forget that.'

Krishna said nothing and turned away. Rukmi stumbled as he dragged himself to the river to bathe his wounds; to wash his half-shaven head. Then he limped away, humiliated and broken, bearing his shame forever.

Having trounced Rukmi, Krishna and Rukmini left once more in the chariot. The road to Dwarka was lined with people shouting out Krishna's name. As they entered the city, more and more people rushed out to welcome their new queen. The heady tale of Krishna's valiant abduction of the beautiful Rukmini was being narrated over and over again, much to their joy. The air, perfumed and bright with colour, was full of celebration, singing and dancing as Krishna wed Rukmini. The gods in heaven watched as they walked around the sacred fire and took their vows, and suddenly there was a shower of blossoms from the blue sky. People looked up and gasped in wonder but Krishna quietly clasped his bride's hand to his heart and smiled.

He knew she was the chosen one. She was Laxmi born on earth to be his consort. Rukmini gazed up at the blue sky and then touched her beloved Krishna's face. Finally, all the blue shades she had ever seen in her mind were merged into one and she too had blended with them. Her Blue God was now hers forever and ever; for many lives to come.

II

MANDODARI & RAVANA

A Wife's Devotion

'I burn with anguish when we are apart,
When he returns, with jealous fear;
And when I see him, he assaults my heart;
I faint when he is near.
No single moment can I capture bliss,
When he is gone, or when he is here.
What in the world can be more strange than this?
And yet, he is my dear.'

—Amaru

My story is of intense, passionate love and heartbreak. From the time I was born, I was destined to be abandoned. I was Madhura in my last life, the most sought after apsara. I was so proud of my beauty and power that I forgot myself and began lusting after Shiva. Parvati, his wife, came to know of this and, furious with jealousy and rage, cursed me. A supreme goddess's curse is very powerful and I was turned into a frog instantly. Fortunately, my lord Shiva took pity on me and I was born as a girl on earth. My earlier frog-like form compelled me to live in a well and there, in the deep murky waters, I would have lived, unloved and abandoned, but fortune suddenly smiled on me. I was rescued by the great asura king Mayasura and his kind wife, Hema.

I changed from an apsara to a frog to a girl who belonged to no one, and then to a princess. I was named Mandodari. My adoptive parents brought me up with affection and tender care. I had hundreds of maids to take care of me and I only wore the finest jewels and silk clothes. I became an expert in archery and learnt the science of building mansions from my father, who was a great architect.

Despite my lowly birth, I had grown into such a beautiful woman that all the asura princes in our realm began to fight for my hand as soon as I came of age. But my father, the asura king, had great ambitions for me. He searched for my husband far and wide in the asura world and then he chose the mightiest of them all—he chose Ravana.

I was overjoyed. Which girl would not be? I had heard that Ravana was not only the most handsome, the most powerful king of our time, he was a great scholar too. He had mastered the four Vedas at a very young age and possessed a profound knowledge of Ayurveda and astrology. He was highly skilled in music, dance and occult science. Those who had heard him play the veena said they were transported to a magical world. He had composed the renowned Shiva Tandava Stotram in praise of Lord Mahadeva and the great god had given him many boons.

It gladdened my heart that Ravana was a true devotee of Lord Shiva because I knew that in this life too, I would be attached to the great Lord Shiva in some way. I waited eagerly for my wedding day. I thought about Ravana all the time and longed to see him even for a brief moment.

Finally, our wedding day arrived and I was so overwhelmed with joy, I thought I would die. I tried to calm myself down by praying to Lord Shiva. 'Let me be a perfect wife to my husband. Let our love for each other be true and flourish forever,' I chanted. If only I had asked Lord Shiva to give my husband wisdom and good sense that day; or to gift him humility and kindness.

There was great excitement as Ravana flew down to our palace in his golden chariot. Our wedding was the most magnificent ceremony that anybody had ever seen. All the wealth Ravana had taken by force from his half-brother Kubera was put on display and the entire city of Lanka glittered with thousands of lamps like a heavenly abode. The streets were perfumed with the scent of roses. Even the gods in Indralok must have been envious that day of Lanka's magical beauty.

I was bedecked in the finest jewels since my father too wanted to show off his wealth to everyone present. All the great asuras competed with each other to shower priceless gifts on us. I was thrilled to receive such beautiful jewels but my husband did not even look at them.

'What do you need these insignificant, ordinary jewels for? I already have all the best jewels in the three worlds. Just remember, I am the greatest of all kings assembled here. I am the invincible Lankesh. Who can match my splendour?' he said, an arrogant sneer distorting his handsome face.

I should have realized then the kind of man I had married. But I was besotted with him. I could see no faults in this powerful, mesmerizing demon king whom I had been fortunate enough to wed; I loved him with all my heart. He was the only one who mattered in this world. I longed for him day and night. My heart, my body and my soul belonged only to him. I forgot who I was. Nobody but Ravana existed for me. Even when he was not around, I could sense his powerful, thrilling presence and my heart would race with anticipation and joy. I still could not believe that he was my husband and I was his wife.

I did not know that one day this heart of mine would be broken by the very person I loved so much. I only knew that when he looked at me and when he took me in his arms, the world became a magical, glorious place. There was no greater joy for me that to behold this resplendent mighty asura king who was my lord and master. I was a slave to him and I would do anything to retain his love.

My husband started being unfaithful to me a few months after we were wed. Shocked and filled with sorrow, I could not believe it but when I asked him the reason why he had left our marital bed for another woman, he just laughed. His dark eyes gave me a quick, indifferent glance.

'You are the queen of Lanka. Remember that, Mandodari, and be content with that. You are my first and most important wife but, know this, there will be many more. I have to marry several times to form alliances with neighbouring states. That is the way kings expand their territories. You are a princess and you should know that. So stop sobbing like a common, low-born girl. I hate women who cry for no reason,' he said and stormed out of our bedchamber.

All my dreams of true, eternal love were shattered that day but a worse fate awaited not just me but the entire kingdom of Lanka. We were blinded by our wealth and splendour and could not see the dark clouds approaching our kingdom. All I knew was that Lanka, glittering with its golden palaces and untold riches, was the greatest place on earth and I, Mandodari, was its queen.

Ravana roamed the earth, winning battles and bringing back more wealth. Each time he returned victorious, a new woman was with him, but I steeled my heart and pretended not to care. Suddenly showing great generosity, my faithless husband built me my own golden palace with a vast, magnificent garden. Here, in the shade of the trees, I would sit alone and listen to the servants discussing yet another beautiful new woman my husband had brought from another land. After some time, I became used to these affairs. I had been blessed with a son and Meghnada was my entire life now. Soon another two sons were born to me. I was content and at peace with myself. I still loved Ravana with all my heart but I knew that I was one of the many women he loved. That was his nature and I had to accept it. What other choice did I have? I told myself each day that I was Ravana's chief wife, his first wife, and to be happy with just that.

Fate, once again, was watching me with cruel eyes, waiting to create havoc. The long journey to our destruction began the day Ravana received an invitation to a swayamvar being held by King Janaka of Mithila. His daughter Sita, famed for her beauty, had come of age, and the king invited my husband, along with many other kings and princes, for her swayamvar. He knew Ravana had several wives already but that did not seem to matter. What mattered was that he was the most powerful ally any king could wish for.

Ravana, very pleased with himself to have received an invitation, set out for Mithila at once. This was going to be no ordinary swayamvar. The suitor had to lift and string a mighty bow that belonged to Lord Shiva. My husband was very confident that only he could achieve this task and, arrogant and flushed with pride, he could not stop smiling. Though he often travelled to fight battles and came back with trophies, this time, my heart was filled with anxiety and fear. Before he climbed into the chariot, I begged him not to go to Mithila.

'We have a growing family. Lanka is one of the richest kingdoms. We don't need an alliance with Mithala.'

'Who cares about Mithala? I must get Mahadeva's bow for myself. It rightfully belongs to me and only me,' he said, getting agitated and angry with me.

'You know you will have to marry Sita too. Maybe that is the reason you are going to Mithala,' I said.

'Your jealousy will never end, will it?' he shouted and left with a furious look at me.

The palace waited for their king to return with Shiva's bow and a new wife—Sita. I waited too, fearful and restless.

I was shocked to hear that my husband, for the first time in his life, was defeated. He could not string the great Lord Shiva's bow and returned home humiliated and ashamed. All the other asuras, who had been jealous of Ravana before, had laughed at his defeat and he could not bear this insult. Later, we heard that a young prince of Ayodhya had not only strung the mighty bow but had broken it. His name was Ram and he was Sita's husband now.

Anger simmered in my husband's heart. Then one day his sister Surpanakha came to the palace, howling with pain, her face mutilated and bleeding.

'Brother, you call yourself a mighty warrior but see what these two boy princes of Ayodhya—Ram and Laxman—have done to your sister. They slashed my face as Ram's wife Sita watched.'

As all the asuras assembled in Lankeshwar's court watched in horror, my entire body began to shiver as if snakes were crawling over me. I began to sob, trying to wipe the blood from Surpanakha's ravaged face. It was a terrible thing to happen to her but I was crying for myself because I knew that the worst was yet to come. For some reason, the name Sita made me tremble with fear. I could not understand why I would hate someone I had never seen.

A gloom fell upon our palace. For weeks, Ravana stayed locked up in his own chamber. He refused to meet me. I pleaded with the guard at his door but my husband did not want to see anyone except his war ministers. I heard the palace servants whispering nervously about bad omens that had been seen all over Lanka.

Then one day my husband came out of his chamber and, without giving me a glance, stormed out of the palace. 'I will take revenge for this. Those two boys will regret what they have done to my sister,' he shouted. After a few minutes, I saw his flying chariot rise swiftly into the sky and disappear from my vision.

A week passed. It was a strange, eerie time when the birds in the garden stopped singing and the rivers of Lanka began drying up for no reason. The moon was streaked with a crimson red scar as if it were bleeding. Then Lankesh returned. As his pushpak vimana landed in the palace garden, I rushed out to greet him.

Then I stopped. He looked more powerful and more handsome than ever. He was roaring with laughter in a way that I had never seen him laugh before. He seemed to have lost his dignity, his senses. Behind him cowered a young girl, slender and beautiful, her face as delicate as a lotus blossom. 'He has brought Sita back with him,' whispered someone. 'He has abducted Sita from her husband Ram.' For the first time in the history of our land, no one applauded the return of our king.

From then on, the days passed in agony for me. I was distraught, but not just because Ravana had brought another woman to Lanka. This time was it was different. Sita, I had heard, was no ordinary woman, and Ram was no ordinary man. This, I knew in my heart, was the beginning of the end.

I often thought of going to visit Sita in the garden where she was being held prisoner by my husband but then I thought, what would I say to her? I felt guilty for her plight but was helpless to do anything for her. Envy burnt in my heart when I thought about how my husband had lost his mind for her.

He had abducted her to seek revenge for his sister but now he now longed to possess her, despite her refusing him over and over again.

We were soon attacked by Ram's army and within a few days, Lanka became a dead city. The battle raged on and I lost track of how many of our kin died.

In one week, I lost all my three sons. I had no more tears to shed as I saw the countless bodies of our male relatives lying dead on the battlefield. Hundreds of women in every corner of Lanka mourned. Our glorious kingdom now lay in ruins. Our king, our great king, had lost his mind entirely, all because of his ego, his pride and his desire for another man's wife.

During this turbulent time, Sita sat quietly in her secluded garden and prayed all day. When I was told that she was certain her husband would come to rescue her, I had laughed at her stupidity. Who could defeat my great lord; who could defeat the mighty asura king Lankeshwar? But later, as I watched my Lanka being destroyed by Ram's army, I no longer laughed. I just stood silently, watching the destruction as if I were made of stone. I felt nothing. Was it in another lifetime that I had drowned in the river of fire? I could not believe that jealousy and rage had filled the core of my being; that I had hated this young girl with whom my husband was so besotted. Now the name Sita evoked not jealousy but an unspeakable fear in me. It meant the end of my world. It meant the death of my husband, one of the greatest warriors of all three worlds, the most learned of all asura kings; it meant the end of Ravana. His arrogance, his pride and his ego were vanquished forever by Sita's husband Ram.

As I fast unto death, I pray with my feeble breath that in my next life I am Ravana's wife again. Despite all the pain, the anguish and the humiliation I have suffered, I still want him as my husband. I want Ravana, the greatest asura king and warrior, the most devout worshipper of Lord Shiva, to be mine again. The light slowly fades from my dying eyes and I see him. He stands before me, darkly handsome in all his resplendent majesty, my only beloved, my life.

I pray with my dying breath that in my next life Ravana will love no other woman but Mandodari. Then darkness falls as I place my life at his feet and merge into his being.

12

URVASHI & PURURAVAS

Magical Love

'Lost in deep, sweet love,
Cheek leaning on cheek,
We talked
Of whatever came to our minds.
Just as it flowed,
Oh slowly
So slowly,
With our arms twined
Tightly around us
And the hours passed
And we
Did not know it,
Still talking
When the night had gone.'

—Bhavabhuti

When Urvashi gazed upon her reflection in the pond, she would be startled by her own beauty. 'I am perfect but I want a man's admiring, caressing look to feel more beautiful. I must search for a mere mortal to fall in love with me; only a mortal with a frail human heart will adore me with a passion that the gods can never match,' she said and smiled. Her reflection smiled back at her and then the waves rippled over to erase it as she trailed her hand in the cool water. To herself, she said, 'I will find that man who will love me madly. I need no instructions in the art of using my charms to win a man's heart. After all, a lily's scarlet stamens grow untaught and the bee comes freely, wishing to be caught.'

Urvashi was the first amongst the apsaras, the jewel of Indra's court in heaven. These extraordinarily beautiful celestial nymphs emerged when the ocean of milk was being churned by the gods and the demons. They could change their shape as they wished, to make themselves even more alluring, and the gods believed that they could make a man go insane with desire. Urvashi's beauty could enchant the gods, and as for mere mortals, she could slay them with a quick glance. She was considered not only the most beautiful maiden in heaven, but the most talented too.

While Urvashi was the reigning apsara of heaven, King Pururavas was said to be the most handsome and valiant king of his time on earth. And though they came from different worlds it was destined that they should meet, and as soon as they met, they fell in love with each other at first sight.

One fine, misty dawn, when the sun was softly gleaming in the sky, Urvashi, along with a few other celestial nymphs, decided to come down to earth. While they were frolicking about in the woods, picking wild flowers, chasing butterflies and bathing in the river, they were seen by a demon who was lurking behind the trees.

'How beautiful and gorgeous these heavenly nymphs are! I will trap them and make them my slaves. Then all the other demons will envy me,' he said to himself, his eyes glinting with malice as he watched the nymphs singing and dancing around the trees.

Despite being extremely agile and cautious, the nymphs were caught by the demon and trapped in his powerful, gigantic arms. The nymphs, confused and stunned by this sudden attack, forgot their powers and began screaming for help like mortals. King Pururavas, who happened to be passing by, heard this strange wailing noise. He ran towards the sound and spotted the beautiful, unearthly maidens crying for help as they struggled to free themselves from the demon's clutches. The valiant king acted at once. He drew an arrow from his bow with lightning speed and killed the demon in one swift movement.

As soon as the nymphs were set free, they began to shout with joy and danced around the king. They thanked him profusely and then swiftly got into their celestial chariot to fly back to heaven, vowing never to come down to earth again, however tempting the lovely woods and the rivers seemed. 'We thank you, O noble king, for saving us,' they sang in their sweet, musical voices as they stepped into their chariot.

As the chariot hovered in the air for a few fleeting moments, King Pururavas looked up and saw Urvashi—and in that moment his heart was lost forever. He had never seen such an exquisite, enchanting maiden in his life. His heart began to race and every pore of his being now yearned for this heavenly apsara. At the same moment, Urvashi looked down at the handsome, regal man gazing up at her and she too fell in love with him as soon as she set eyes on him. 'He is the one. He is the lover I need,' she thought.

The world seemed to stand still as they continued to gaze at each other. They both knew they could not live without each other though they lived in two different worlds. Urvashi could not leave heaven without incurring Lord Indra's wrath and Pururavas, a mortal man, could not go to heaven while he lived. They held each other's gaze, their eyes brimming with love and despair at the same time. Then the other nymphs, impatient to be gone, forced Urvashi to turn her face away and their chariot swiftly rose in the air and vanished into the sky. Though he could not see Urvashi, Pururavas felt she was still in front of him; he could hear her musical voice singing to him for a long time even after she had disappeared and clouds had darkened the sky.

The king returned to the palace a changed man. Besotted with Urvashi, Pururavas could not eat or sleep. He pined for the beautiful apsara and though he had seen her only for a brief moment, it seemed to him he had loved her all his life; it seemed to him she had come down to earth on that fateful morning only for them to meet each other; to fall in love with each other.

'How can I find her? Will she ever come down to earth again? I cannot live without her. I will give up my life and go to heaven to search for her,' he thought, gazing up at the sky with forlorn eyes. Fortunately for him, Urvashi felt the same way about him and now loved him with all her heart, though he was a mere mortal. 'I need to see him again. I need him not just to feed my vanity but to fulfil my soul. He is the most perfect human I have ever seen. I must go down to earth and be with him.' She knew that this act would be frowned upon by the gods and that she would be cast out of heaven, but she could not help herself. Her passion for Pururavas made her reckless and she decided that she would give herself to him, no matter what happened.

So, one moonlit night, she made herself invisible and flew down to earth. The palace garden was bathed in the silvery light of a brilliant moon and the night jasmine flowers had just opened their petals when Pururavas, who was pacing restlessly in the garden, saw Urvashi walking towards him.

For a few bewildering moments he thought he was dreaming and this gorgeous vision of beauty was a figment of his fevered, love-crazed imagination. Then she came towards him, floating on a beam of shimmering, silvery light, surrounded by fireflies, her enchanting face glowing in the moonlight. They gazed at each other and then she touched his face with her hands. King Pururavas thought he would die, unable to bear such intense happiness, but he was also afraid that this was a dream and he would wake up and find himself alone again.

Then Urvashi spoke in a soft, musical voice. 'I have come down to earth from heaven so that we can be together. I will be yours, O king, but you must agree to these three conditions I will put before you.

'First, I will bring down two lambs from heaven. They will always live with me. You must see that no harm ever comes to them.

'Second, I will eat and drink nothing except for pure clarified butter.

'Third, and the most important condition I place before you, is that you must never appear before me naked.

'Take heed, O noble king. If you disregard any of these conditions, I will leave you at once and you will never see me again.'

Pururavas, overjoyed that this exquisite celestial nymph had agreed to be his wife, bowed his head and said, 'I agree to every condition of yours. You have made me the happiest man on earth. You can ask me for anything and I will give it to you.'

'I ask for nothing, noble king. Just remember these three conditions of mine,' she said, stepping into his arms. Pururavas felt his heart would burst with the flood of happiness that swept over him as he held her in a tight embrace.

From that day onwards, Urvashi and Pururavas lived together in total bliss and happiness. Though she had been thrown out of heaven for marrying a mortal, Urvashi was very content to live on earth since she knew she was loved as she had never been loved before. 'My life with him is perfect; my happiness when I lie in his arms overflows like a river in flood,' she thought to herself.

The gods and gandharvas of heaven admired her greatly, they loved the way she sang and danced, or played the lute for them, but not one of them loved her with all their soul like Pururavas did. Though she was a celestial nymph with magical powers, King Pururavas treated her gently and tenderly as if were was a fragile being and granted her every wish. He also treated her two lambs with great affection and was very careful never to appear before her naked.

Together they roamed the palace gardens, mostly at night since Urvashi loved the moonlight. Pururavas plucked fragrant jasmine flowers and wove them into her hair. He washed her feet with cool water from the spring and then gently caressed her face, whispering words of love in a soft voice. They lay together all night in a bower of flowers and only the moon could see them thus, clasped in a loving embrace.

Years passed on earth, but in heaven earthly years were just a few days. Urvashi was greatly missed by everyone at Indra's heavenly court. She had been the most beautiful of the apsaras; the most admired nymph since she sang and danced better than all the other heavenly nymphs. The gandharvas, her erstwhile companions and friends, who missed her more than anyone else, became very jealous of her joyous life on earth.

'How can she live with an ordinary human with no powers and yet be so happy? We have to get her back to heaven somehow,' they said, looking down angrily at the happy couple as they walked about, arm in arm, in the palace gardens.

So the gandharvas, who were highly skilled in the magical arts and knew how to cast all kinds of spells, came up with a plan. Two of the cleverest ones quietly flew down to earth on a dark, moonless night. They stole into the palace and, moving as silently as shadows, they entered the king's chamber where Urvashi and Pururavas slept. The two small lambs were sleeping peacefully near Urvashi. One of the gandharvas swooped down and quickly picked up the lambs and rose into the air. Startled by the animals' bleating, Pururavas woke up at once. As soon as he saw that someone was carrying the lambs away, he leapt up. He knew he had to save them since he had promised Urvashi he would always protect her lambs. So he grabbed his sword and charged out of the room. In his haste to catch the thief, he forgot to drape himself with his royal robe. As he ran in pursuit of the thief, a streak of lightning, created by the gandharvas, flashed through the palace rooms. Exactly at that moment, Urvashi woke up. She saw that her lambs had vanished and her husband was running across the room, bathed in a bright, unreal light, totally naked.

In one quick, silvery moment, Urvashi vanished.

King Pururavas was stunned. He ran around the palace, heartbroken, desolate and bewildered. He could not understand how such a terrible thing could have happened. 'In one terrible, cruel moment, she has gone. How could this happen?' he cried. They had been so happy together and he had taken every care to keep his promises to her. He had never broken any of the three conditions Urvashi had placed before him till that one fateful night.

'My life is not worth living. Urvashi, please return to me and save me from this torment. I beseech you to save me from this hell,' he sobbed.

As the days passed, King Pururavas was stricken with such deep sorrow that his people thought he would die of grief, but he managed to live. He wandered around, constantly searching for his beloved in every corner of the earth, though deep in his heart he knew she had gone back to heaven. 'Yet I must continue to look for my beloved. There is nothing else that is meaningful in my life now,' he said to himself.

Then one day, weary and his heart aching with sadness, he sat down beside the river Jamuna to rest his tired limbs, and that was when he saw Urvashi once again. She was bathing in the river and she called him to her, a gentle smile on her radiant face.

Startled and overcome with happiness, the king could not speak and just stood silently, looking at his wife. He could not believe it was her. For a few minutes he wondered if some demon was playing a trick on him or trying to cast a spell on him, but then Urvashi reached out for him. As soon as she touched him, he knew she was real and his heart leapt with joy.

'We cannot live together since that is not our destiny but you can come and be with me for one night every year. I will give you a son. That will be my gift to you,' she whispered, brushing her lips over his cheeks. 'I will never forget our life together. You were a most gentle and caring lover. You made me so happy. I will always remember how you adorned my hair with flowers, how we sat in the garden on moonlit nights, swinging on the flower-covered swing you had made for me. O king, you will always be in my heart and I will sing to you every night from heaven,' she said, and disappeared into the sky.

King Pururavas sat quietly on the riverbank for a long time, gazing up at the sky, hoping he would catch another glimpse of Urvashi, but all he saw were a few clouds floating in the vast empty sky. Though he was terribly sad that he could meet his beloved wife only once a year, Pururavas consoled himself with the thought that he would have a son from her one day. At night he would hear her sweet voice singing to him from the skies and it filled him with a desperate longing to be with her again. He counted the days, the hours and the minutes till they could be together again.

For the next five years they met once a year and finally the gods, impressed with Pururavas's true devotion to his wife and his pure love for her, offered him a boon.

'O noble, loyal king, choose what you want and we will grant it to you,' they said.

'All I want is to live with my wife in peace,' he said. The gods agreed and allowed them to live together. Urvashi was delighted. 'You must also pray to the gandharvas and they will gift me to you. They will never try to take me away from you, if you please them. Then we can be together forever,' she said, her eyes gleaming with joy.

King Pururavas did exactly as she had asked him. He performed many fire sacrifices and sat and prayed for long periods. The gandharvas were very pleased with his devotion. Though they were sorry to part with their favourite apsara, they decided to let her live on earth. They knew they could call her to heaven whenever they wanted to.

Once King Pururavas's life on earth ended, he too went to live in heaven. Now Urvashi and he were together forever and the gods gave them their blessings.

'Your devotion and love for each other is true and pure. We give you our blessings and you both shall never be separated again.'

Thousands of years passed but people on earth never forgot their love story. Many believe that Urvashi, also known as 'dawn', is loved intensely by the sun, who is like Pururavas, but their love lasts only for an hour at sunrise. She is a wisp of the morning mist and must vanish when the sun grows strong. Dawn is happy because she knows she is truly loved by the sun during the brief hour of sunrise and so she is content to disappear when the sun rises higher in the sky. Thus their love for each other is renewed each dawn and they are immersed in total bliss in that brief, magical hour of love. Legend has it that their love for each other will endure as long as the sun rises in the sky.

13

SAMJNA & SURYA

An Overpowering Love

'Living here
Far away,
I am yours.
Living there
Far away,
You are mine.
Love is not made of bodies only,
Deep in our hearts
Is where
We are one.'

—Shri Kashinath Sharma,
Subhasita Ratna Bhandagara

The rains had washed clean the vast, heavenly garden, and the luxuriant flowering trees, now bathed in dawn's golden light, sparkled as if covered in jewels. A cool, scented breeze floated around as Samjna plucked a parijata blossom and inhaled its sweet fragrance. 'Whom shall I marry, tell me?' she whispered to the tree, gently touching the flower-laden branches, swaying in the breeze. A passing gandharva had told her once that the parijata tree could foretell a young maiden's future husband's name. Samjna and her sisters often came to the tree to ask about their future husbands but so far the tree had not responded.

When their father, Vishwakarma, heard about this, he was very angry. 'You are very foolish, girls. The tree will not speak to you ever. Only I, your father, can tell you your future husband's name,' he said, and ordered the girls not to circle the tree every day.

Samjna, always obedient and respectful of her father's wishes, stopped asking the tree but in her mind the question kept running, like a bubbling stream. In the silence of the night, when all was quiet, she gazed at the brilliant stars in the sky and whispered to herself, 'Will my husband be handsome or plain? Will he be a lesser god or just an ordinary, mortal man? Will he be valiant and brave or an ascetic, silent being? Will he come to wed me riding on a white steed or on a bedecked elephant?'

Samjna had no idea that her father had been searching for a perfect husband for her for many years and had already rejected many lesser gods and mortals. He had briefly considered a few major gods but none of them seemed suitable to him.

'I want a god of whom the universe is in awe. Our daughter is perfect and she should marry a perfect heavenly being,' he often said to his wife. She did not answer him and silently walked away each time he said this to her. She was beginning to get worried that this beautiful daughter of theirs would never find a husband since her father kept rejecting each and every suitor.

Then one day at dawn, when Vishwakarma was doing his prayers, he gazed at the sun, which was slowly and gracefully rising on the horizon. He chanted his prayers as he offered water to the huge orange and gold disc shining brilliantly in the sky. The entire universe seemed to stand still, as if paying their respects to the majestic rising sun. Gradually, the golden rays began to spread their light as the sun rose higher and higher to adorn the sky like a massive, shimmering orb. Every living being on earth raised their heads to greet the sun and then bowed to salute the all benevolent god. Suddenly, a thought came into Vishwakarma's mind as he bowed his head, and he gave a jubilant cry of joy. 'Why have I not thought of this before?' he said loudly to himself.

'I want the mighty Sun God to wed my daughter,' he said, bowing low to pay his respects to the fiery golden sun adorning the sky.

Viswakarma, the supreme architect of the gods, decided then and there that Samjna, his most beautiful and accomplished daughter, would marry the great God Surya. 'He will be the perfect husband for her. Surya has a wondrous aura no other being possesses and he is endowed with great virtue. His wealth is unimaginable and he will live forever and ever. Samjna will lead a happy, prosperous live with him,' he thought, very pleased with his decision.

He rushed to Surya's palace in the sky and, after listing Samjna's virtues and describing her beauty at great length, he offered her hand to him.

The glorious god of sunlight and universal warmth agreed at once. 'Yes, I will be very happy to marry your exquisitely beautiful and noble daughter. I have often seen her strolling in your garden and wished I could make her my wife one day. I know that she is renowned for her beauty, virtue and ascetic powers. Please make all the arrangements for our wedding. We must invite all the gods and goddesses and the gandharvas and apsaras too. The moon, the stars, the planets and the entire universe should celebrate our wedding.'

'Yes, my lord. I will plan such a magnificent ceremony that everyone in heaven will be amazed and they will talk about your glorious wedding for years to come,' said Vishwakarma.

Surya nodded his fiery, golden head and went away laughing and shimmering in delight.

When Samjna was told that she was to marry the great god Surya, she too was overjoyed. 'My father has chosen the perfect husband for me. Surya is a mighty god. He is the great luminous benefactor for the entire universe. His glory will reflect on me and I shall become an important woman too. I shall live in a huge, golden palace in the sky and have all the riches heaven can offer. How my sisters will envy me,' she thought, smiling and dancing with glee. Then she stopped herself. 'I must not get carried away by this good fortune and become too proud. I must continue to meditate and be calm. I will now pray to the gods with deeper commitment and show them my eternal gratitude,' she said, and she sat down quietly and reflected on her future husband's virtues.

Later, when she went to thank her father, he touched her head gently and said, 'It took a long time but finally I have found the best husband for you, my daughter. We are blessed that you shall become his wife. You must obey him and be a good wife to him. Surya is a kind, benevolent god but he contains within himself immense power and has a fiery temper. I don't want any complaints from him about your behaviour.'

'Father, you have found me a most wonderful, divine husband. Why should I ever give you cause for grief? I will be the best wife for Surya, you wait and see. You will hear nothing but praise from him about me. I will make you proud, dear father,' she said and touched her father's feet. He gave her his blessings and said, 'We must start preparing for a grand, opulent ceremony. I am going to put all my creative skills into planning a glorious wedding for you. Go, daughter, and choose your wedding saree. There is no time to lose. Everything should be perfect. My daughter is marrying the Sun God and it is the most joyous occasion for our family. I want everyone in heaven to rejoice with us and remember forever the splendid wedding Vishwakarma held for his beloved daughter.'

Samjna ran to the palace seamstress and together they sat down to weave her wedding saree. To colour the threads, they took glinting bits of silver from the stars, shimmering blue from the heavenly rivers, rich dark blue from the night, deep crimson from the celestial blossoms and emerald green from the evergreen trees that grew in Indra's garden. Dressed by her mother in this resplendent saree and bedecked with rare, precious gems from the depths of the oceans on her wedding day, Samjna was the most beautiful bride the heavens had seen in a long time.

Goddess Laxmi blessed her with immense wealth, Goddess Saraswati with the gift of vast knowledge and lyrical speech, and Lord Shiva himself came down from the mountains to place his hand on her head in blessing. Lord Vishnu gifted her with blue lotus blossoms that would never lose their fragrance and Vayu, the god of wind, sent a white steed that could run at lightning speed.

When Samjna placed a garland of rare blossoms around Surya's neck, all the gandharvas in heaven began singing and the entire universe burst into song. Flowers cascaded down on the wedded couple and brilliant rays of light of every hue circled them as Surya led his bride around the sacred fire seven times.

After the wedding ceremony was over, Samjna was led to a golden chariot with seven white horses and she flew away to live in her husband's magnificent golden palace in the clouds.

For the first few years of her marriage, Samjna was very happy and sang softly to herself every morning as she strolled in the vast gardens of the palace. Birds sang with her and the sound of rainclouds murmuring in the distance soothed her body and mind.

She often thought about her home and wondered what her sisters, married to lesser gods and ordinary mortals, were doing. She longed to visit them but she was afraid to ask the

Sun God for permission to go home. 'He might get annoyed and think I am not happy with him. He might think I have a fickle and restless nature. I shall just live here quietly and forget about them. I am happy with my husband and my three children.'

Samjna and Surya's three children were called Manu, Yama and Yami. They were strong, clever and handsome and the Sun God was very proud of them. He often took them with him as he rode across the sky in his chariot pulled by seven horses. He loved his wife with a true passion and tried his best to please her. He brought her gifts of precious gems from various corners of the earth and ordered the gandharvas to sing for her every morning.

'I have found a lovely, perfect wife in Samjna. She is so graceful and gentle and looks after my every need,' he often said to the other gods. All the heavenly beings praised her too and wished them good fortune forever.

But an envious eye, lurking in a dark corner of the universe, fell upon them and their happy union began to fragment bit by bit. At first she did not notice it but Samjna gradually began to grow more and more restless and unhappy. She was bewildered and confused and could not understand why this feeling of unease was creeping upon her. It was as if a poisonous snake was coiling itself around her limbs, draining the life out of her. How happy she had been just a year ago! How she had basked in her divine husband's radiant glow and flourished under his loving care. But now everything seemed to have changed suddenly like the day changes to night.

Her great husband's magnificent aura, that had so impressed her once with its brilliance, now pierced her like a thousand arrows. His very presence now began to hurt her. She began to find his golden rays too harsh and they burnt her body. Her skin, her throat and her entire being felt parched and thirsty all the time. She often gasped for breath and longed to hide in a cool, dark corner. Her only solace was secretly plunging herself in a pool of cold water in the heavenly garden at night.

The splendid, golden palace that she had once admired so much now began to oppress her. 'How proud I was of my vast mansion in the sky. Everyone envied me this golden palace. What if they saw me now, cowering behind pillars?' she thought, a deep sadness flooding over her.

She roamed the palace sobbing quietly. Sunlight blazed into every corner, following her all day, and she desperately searched for a dark corner where she could take shelter from its brilliance.

Whenever Surya, resplendent, all-powerful and emitting thousands of sunbeams, came near her, her skin began to hurt and her eyes filled with tears. She loved her husband dearly so she had tolerated his intense heat and light all these years, but now she could no longer stand it. 'I am afraid I will be blinded by his intense light soon,' she thought, and that very day, she fainted as soon as she beheld his glowing, shining image coming towards her.

That night, she decided to leave him. 'I know what I am doing is wrong and I will be blamed by my father and everyone else but I cannot live like this. Surya's fierce, scorching light will burn me to death. I have to escape his brilliance however much I love him,' Samjna thought, her heart breaking with sorrow at the thought of leaving her husband who had been so kind and loving to her.

'I need to go away from him to save myself. I must leave him but I do not want him to feel lonely. I must make sure he is taken care of and never feels my absence. My three children too must be looked after well after I go,' she thought.

So, with meticulous care, Samjna created a shadow image of herself and gave it life. She had learnt the art of magical, creative skills from her father Vishwakarma and knew exactly how to form an image that would look and speak like herself. She named her double, this exact image of herself, Chaya. After secretly installing Chaya in her place, Samjna fled to the high Himalayan mountains. She roamed around till she found a quiet, remote mountain peak and there she lay down on the soft, cool dew-drenched grass and she wept in relief.

'O my husband. I will miss you with all my heart. But I could not bear your scorching rays and your intense burning light. I need to be in the shade. Please forgive me and be happy with Chaya. She will look after all your needs just like I did. I taught her everything before I left. My loving gaze will be upon you. Be happy and at peace, my lord,' she whispered, and then she sat down under the shade of a rock to meditate in the silent wilderness.

Surya lived happily with his false wife Chaya and did not suspect for a single moment that she was not his true wife

Samjna. Years passed and they had three children together. Chaya was not very kind to Samjna's children and treated them very cruelly. She took care to hide this from Surya but one day he caught her snatching food from Yama's mouth.

'What kind of mother allows her child to starve?' thought Surya, shocked at Chaya's behaviour.

'Why do you treat him like this? Are you not his mother? Who are you, wicked woman?' he shouted, suddenly realizing that something was amiss. This woman could not be his kind and loving Samjna. He thundered at her until she confessed.

'I am Chaya. Your wife Samjna created me and put me in her place when she went away,' said Chaya, cowering in fear.

The Sun God roared with anger and threw Chaya out of his palace at once. Then he stood quietly, unable to believe that his loving Samjna had left him. His heart was shattered with grief and hurt. 'Samjna. How could you do this? I loved you with all my being. We were so blissfully happy together. What did I do wrong? Why did you leave me?' he cried, tears of molten fire running down his noble face.

'I have to find her. I will concentrate all my powers and send my light into the universe to find her. She must come back to me. I need my beloved wife,' he said, and sat down to meditate. A hushed silence fell upon the golden palace as Surya concentrated all his energies into searching for his wife. His rays penetrated deep into the netherworld, high into the sky and beyond but they could not find her. After a few months had passed, suddenly, Samjna's image flashed in his mind's eye. He saw that she had turned herself into a mare to hide from the world and sat meditating on a remote mountain peak.

Thrilled to have found her at last, the great Sun God turned himself into a horse and flew as swift as the wind on his magical wings to meet his wife. 'O, my heart. We shall soon be together. How I long to see your beautiful face, feel your gentle touch,' he whispered as he raced across the sky.

Samjna was lost in deep meditation. She sat still, totally immersed in a universe far beyond the real world, and did not hear the sound of the horse galloping towards her. Then a warm, shimmering light pierced through her mind and she opened her eyes. For a few moments she just stared at the majestic stallion standing quietly before her. Then a voice spoke, pulling her out of her stupor. She recognized the deep, powerful voice of her husband. Her heart began to race. She suddenly realized how much she had missed him; how much she wanted to be with him.

'My beloved, I have finally found you. Why did you leave me? I am so desolate and lost without you by my side. Tell me, why did you abandon our three children and your husband? What did I do to upset you?' asked Surya.

Samjna remained silent. Years of silent meditation had made her lose the power of speech and she did not know what to say to her husband.

'I understand now that you were unhappy with me. But tell me the reason why. What did I do wrong? I must know that otherwise I will just roam on this mountain peak for years, waiting for your answer,' said the Sun God as his eyes filled with tears.

Samjna, unable to bear her husband's distress, forced herself to speak.

'Forgive me, my beloved husband, for leaving you. You are not to blame. You were a loving, kind husband and no maiden in heaven could wish for a better lord and master,' she whispered.

'Then why did you leave me? Why did you install an image of yourself and make me believe she was you? Chaya could never replace you in my heart. I was fooled by her till now. Why did you deceive me like this?' asked Surya in an agitated voice.

Samjna took a deep breath. She knew she had to tell him the truth. He deserved to know since he had done no wrong. She bowed her mare's head and began to speak in a clear, soft voice. 'You are a great god. The entirety of heaven is resplendent because of you. The universe revolves around your glorious self. You are incomparable and omnipotent, my lord. I was so fortunate to have you as my husband. It is my fault that I could not live with you. Your splendid, all-pervading light blinded me. Your intense, forceful heat burnt my skin. I had to escape. I worship and adore you but I cannot live with you. I am oppressed by your heat,' said Samjna.

'I understand your plight now. Why did you not speak to me earlier? I would have done something to help you,' said Surya.

'What could you do, my lord? You are the great Sun God and the entire universe depends on your heat and light,' said Samjna, her voice filled with sadness. Now that she heard his voice after so many years, she longed to be with him.

They both remained silent for a few moments. The wind stopped blowing and the clouds in the sky stood absolutely still. The gods from heaven watched the beautiful, regal horse and mare standing together in the vast, lonely wilderness. They blessed them both and in a flash of a second, the pair moved towards each other. Brought closer, Samjna and Surya's love for each other now burst forth like a mountain spring, and together they galloped along the mountainside.

After a year had passed, Surya once again implored Samjna to return. 'You have to come back with me to heaven. We will find some way to be together,' he said.

Samjna, too, wanted to go back to her home in the clouds. She wanted to be with her husband and her children once again. Suddenly she thought of her father, the gifted architect of the gods. 'Surely my father will think of something. Let us go to him at once,' she said. Together they rushed to Vishwakarma's palace.

Vishwakarma was not very pleased to see his daughter since he had heard that she had abandoned her husband and her children but when he saw Surya with her, he greeted them politely.

'Help us, father. I am sorry for what I did but you must understand that I could not live with my lord's excessive light and heat,' said Samjna.

Her father, moved by her plight, nodded, and touched her head gently. 'No one realized what you have been through. I will help you, dear daughter,' he said.

Then he bowed to the Sun God and said, 'If you grant me permission, my lord, I will make some minor adjustments to your great self.'

Surya, keen to do anything to please his wife, agreed at once.

Vishwakarma brought out his machines and, with meticulous care, he trimmed the edges of the massive, golden disc around Surya. He could only pare an eighth of the great god's form but that seemed enough for Samjna. With the slivers of energy-charged gold that were left over when he cut the Sun God's immense form, Vishwakarma crafted Visnu's famous Sudarshan Chakra—the most powerful weapon on earth, Shiva's brilliant Trishul and Devi's demon-destroying disc.

Surya, now reduced in intensity, went back to his golden palace in the clouds to live happily with Samjna. Every day at dawn, all the beings of heaven and earth saw Surya's wife travel across the sky with her loving husband in their golden chariot, never to be parted again.

14

SHAKUNTALA & DUSHYANT

Love Lost and Regained

'Even a man who is content
Glimpses something
Or a hair of sound
Touches him
And his heart overflows
With a strange longing
He does not recognize.
Then it must be that
He is remembering
In a place out of reach
A form he has loved
In a life before this
The impression of that love is still there
Within him
Waiting.'

—Kalidasa, 'Waking'

The light was changing swiftly and Dushyant could barely see the path ahead. The king of Hastinapur had been out hunting since dawn and, chasing after a deer, he had come deep into the forest, leaving his retinue far behind. Then suddenly, he caught a fleeting glimpse of the deer as it leapt into a clump of trees. The king, an expert hunter, raised his bow and arrow but before he could release the arrow, a voice spoke from the green shadows.

'O noble king. Spare the life of the innocent deer. He belongs to the Sage Kanva. All creatures of the forest take shelter at his ashram. It is a sacred grove of trees and no bird or animal is ever harmed here,' said a sage, stepping forward from the shadows.

'I beg your pardon, sir. I did not know this was an ashram,' said King Dushyant. 'I would like to pay my respects to the great sage. Please take me to him.'

The holy man pointed to a narrow path through the dense vegetation and said, 'Follow me but kindly put your bow and arrow away.'

In a short while they reached a clearing in the forest where a few small thatched huts stood. Flowering creepers climbed over tall trees and deer were roaming around, happily nibbling at the shrubs that surrounded the huts. The gentle, murmuring sound of a flowing stream could be heard nearby. The scented breeze and the shimmering green light filtering through the trees created a serene atmosphere of peace and tranquility. The grove was a place of immense calm and the king was overcome with a deep feeling of peace and contentment he had never experienced before.

Then he saw her.

Graceful and slender with gleaming, dark hair cascading down her back like a rain-filled cloud, the girl turned her gaze towards him shyly. She bowed her head and said in a soft, sweet voice, 'Welcome to our humble ashram, sir.

My father, Sage Kanva, is away, but please rest here a while. I will fetch some fruits for you,' she said.

For a few moments, King Dushyant could not speak. He kept staring at the girl, completely mesmerized by her rare beauty. When the girl went into one of the huts, the king turned towards the sage who had brought him to the ashram and asked, 'Who is she? What is this apsara doing in this remote ashram?'

'She, indeed, is a daughter of an apsara. Her mother Menaka was sent to earth by Indra to disturb the meditation of Sage Vishwamitra. She was born of their union but Menaka went back to heaven, leaving her baby daughter behind. Sage Vishwamitra too did not want this child and cast her away. One day, Sage Kanva was roaming in the forest and found this abandoned child, living with the Shakun birds. The birds were feeding and protecting her. He adopted her and named her Shakuntala,' said the sage.

King Dushyant decided to spend a few days in the ashram and sent word to his retinue to go back to the capital. Shakuntala was secretly delighted but did not say anything. She had fallen in love with the king as soon as she had seen him but was too shy and timid to speak to him about her feelings. He was a great king and she was just an ordinary girl living in an ashram; how could she ever dream of marrying such a man? She did not know that King Dushyant had already made up his mind to make her his wife. She was the most beautiful woman he had ever seen and her sweet, innocent nature had won his heart.

Soon enough, the king asked Shakuntala to marry him. Shakuntala was overjoyed but she felt it would be the right thing to do to wait for her father to return before they were wed.

'My father is away, my lord. I cannot marry you without his permission. We must wait till he returns,' she said, even though they both did not know when her father would return.

King Dushyant, always used to getting his way, smiled as he took Shakuntala's hand.

'Why should we wait when we both love each other so truly? True love is such a rare and precious gift. We must make this gift of our love to each other. That is the right thing to do. We will marry in the gandharva way by exchanging garlands. Your father will be very pleased once he knows that you have become my queen,' said the king. He turned her face gently towards him and said in a soft voice, 'I love you as I have never loved any woman before. Be my wife, Shakuntala, my beloved. I cannot wait. Marry me today before the sun sets. We belong to each other. It was destiny that I should come to this remote part of the forest and we should meet. I am certain even the gods wish that we should be united in wedlock.'

His loving words were as sweet as honey and Shakuntala's heart leapt with joy. Though she felt a faint twinge of worry, she could not resist the handsome, noble king. His love for her seemed true. Her entire body and soul wanted to belong to him. She agreed to marry him immediately because she too did not want to wait.

The people of the ashram were overjoyed when they heard the king was going to wed Shakuntala. The women dressed Shakuntala in a simple saree for the wedding. Her only ornaments were wild flowers yet she looked as beautiful as an apsara. Everyone began to celebrate by singing and dancing as the king and Shakuntala exchanged garlands. Peacocks danced around the couple and the deer came out of hiding to watch them.

After the simple gandharva ceremony, Shakuntala and King Dushyant were now husband and wife. The happy couple began to live in the ashram hut, blissfully lost in their own world of love and passion. Shakuntala had never known such love and she was certain that she had done the right thing by marrying the king. 'I am so fortunate to be married to this noble king,' she told herself.

A few weeks passed and then one day a messenger from the palace came to the ashram and asked to meet the king. King Dushyant looked very serious and worried as he talked to the messenger and then he turned to Shakuntala and said, 'I need to get back to the palace. Some urgent war strategy has to be worked out at once. You stay here safely till my ministers come to fetch you, my queen. I hate to leave you behind but I must go. Take this ring of mine. You must always wear it. I shall send for you soon and then you will always be by my side.'

Shakuntala watched her husband walk away from her. Her heart was heavy with sorrow. She was desolate and deeply unhappy that he had to leave but she remained quiet. She did not want to share her pain with anyone. Her husband would soon send for her. 'And then we will be together forever,' she consoled herself. 'Our precious time together was so fleeting. The days seemed to pass like a few minutes. When will I see him again?' she thought, crying softly.

She longed for the king day and night. She could think of nothing else. The deer sat near her all day, trying to comfort her since they could feel her sadness. Shakuntala watched the forest path constantly, hoping and praying she would see the king's ministers coming to fetch her.

One day, Sage Durvasa, who was famed for his fiery temper, came by the ashram. He called out for some water but Shakuntala was lost in thought about her husband and did not hear him. She sat quietly watching the forest path. Her mind was far away. King Dushyant's noble face loomed in front of her eyes as if she were in a dream. The sage called again but she did not reply.

Enraged, the sage cursed her. 'Whoever you are thinking about will forget you, just as you have forgotten your duties to a sage.' His loud, angry voice shocked Shakuntala out of her reverie and she suddenly saw the sage. The words of his terrible curse were still hanging in the air. She fell at his feet in despair. 'O great sage! Forgive me. I will never behave like this again. Let me serve you some fruit. Let me fetch you some cool water.'

Once Sage Durvasa had calmed down, he decided to forgive Shakuntala by changing the curse slightly. 'The person who has forgotten you will remember you when he sees any object he has given you,' he said before leaving.

Months went past. Shakuntala waited but no one came from the palace to fetch her. She grew more pensive and sad each day. The king seemed to have forgotten all about her. When her father returned and was told about everything that had happened in his absence, he decided to send Shakuntala to the king's palace along with some sages from the ashram. 'Go live happily with your husband. Go claim your rightful place as his queen,' said the sage as he gave Shakuntala his blessings. He was sad to see his beloved daughter go away from him but he knew that her rightful place was with her husband. The entire ashram fell silent and even the birds and deer sat quietly as they watched Shakuntala leave.

After walking for a few hours through the forest, the group came upon a swiftly flowing river. 'Let us stop and rest for a while. We can bathe here,' said one of the sages. The water was fresh and cool and soothed their tired limbs. Shakuntala swam in the water, her mind filled with happy thoughts. 'I will be with my beloved soon. How shall I greet him? What will he say when he sees me? How joyous our meeting will be after so long,' she thought and blushed. She was so engrossed in thinking about her husband that she did not notice that the ring had slipped from her finger. The precious jewel, her only gift from her royal husband, was carried away by the river's swift waters.

The group left the river refreshed and resumed walking towards the capital city of Hastinapur where King Dushyant ruled. When they reached the palace, they were presented before him in his glittering court. King Dushyant politely asked them to be seated and asked after Sage Kanva's welfare. Shakuntala lifted her face to gaze upon her husband, her eyes brimming with love. He looked at her in admiration but then looked away to talk to his ministers. The curse had worked. He had not recognized her at all. He had forgotten all about her.

Shakuntala's eyes filled with tears as she looked at the king's face, so loved and familiar and yet so indifferent. 'This is Shakuntala. Your wife, sire,' said one of the sages.

'My wife? I have never seen this beautiful lady before in my life,' said the king. The courtiers looked surprised too.

'Please, sire, have you forgotten our wedding in Sage Kanva's ashram? You gave me your ring,' said Shakuntala, stepping forward, not caring if she was being too bold.

'I don't remember giving any woman a ring. Who are you and what are you doing in my court? What ring are you talking about?' asked King Dushyant in a cold, distant voice.

'This is the ring you gave me after you wed me, my lord,' said Shakuntala in a trembling voice. She raised her hand to show him the ring and then gave a cry of dismay. There was no ring on her finger.

How could she have lost such a precious thing? Shakuntala, distraught with grief, began to sob quietly. She had lost the only token of his love. What should she do now?

'What ring?' asked the king again in an irritated voice. The courtiers began to mutter angrily too. Who was this strange, bold woman? How dare she accuse their king of betrayal?

As Shakuntala stood crying quietly, the sages who had come with her tried once again, to convince the king that Shakuntala was indeed his wife. 'You did marry her in our ashram. You exchanged garlands in the gandharva way. O king. Accept her as your wife. Give her shelter in your palace.'

King Dushyant got up from his throne and, without looking at Shakuntala, strode away in a rage. His ministers came forward at once and spoke to the sages.

'You have made our king very angry. We humbly beg you to go away. Do not waste his time. He has many important matters to discuss in his court,' they said, and the sages were politely but firmly escorted out of the palace. As Shakuntala hid in one corner, unsure of what to do, a priest felt sorry for the great Sage Kanva's daughter and offered to give her shelter. He could see that she was with child. In her sorrow, Shakuntala had agreed to go with him. As they were walking away from the palace, there was a sudden flash of light and a celestial being swept down from the sky and carried Shakuntala away. It was her mother Menaka, who had come to rescue her daughter.

Months passed by and one day in the marketplace there was a great uproar. A fisherman had been arrested when the guards found him with a signet ring that had the king's seal. 'How did you get this ring?' they demanded. The fisherman explained that he had caught a huge fish and when he cut it open, he had found this ring in its stomach. When the guards placed him under arrest, the fisherman insisted on telling his story to the king.

As soon as King Dushyant saw the ring presented by the fisherman, memories of the past flooded over him. The memories of Shakuntala that had been erased by the curse now came rushing back. He remembered the days of love and bliss in the ashram; he remembered his lost love.

'Shakuntala. My beloved wife. How could I have forgotten you? O! My gentle Shakuntala! Why did I let you go?' he cried, his heart filled with regret at what he had done. 'Go and find the priest who gave her shelter. Go at once,' he commanded his soldiers

The priest was found and presented in the palace soon after. He told the king how an apsara had flown down from heaven and carried Shakuntala away. When he heard this, King Dushyant sank into deep despair. 'Will I ever see her again? How will I find her?' He was devastated with grief as he thought about his wife; his beautiful Shakuntala whom he had wronged so cruelly. He prayed constantly that he would find her one day.

A few years passed and then one day King Dushyant was asked by the gods to help in their war against the demons. A massive battle took place and the demons were finally defeated. The king was victorious but still unhappy and sad about his lost love. He was returning home in a flying chariot that belonged to the gods when, suddenly, the chariot stopped and set him down in the middle of a lonely forest.

'What is this strange place? Why have you brought me here?' he asked, but the charioteer flew away, leaving the king behind. The king walked for a while and then he came to a meadow filled with flowers and sweetly scented herbs. A small child, unusually handsome, was playing with a lion cub. The king was amazed to see how brave and unafraid the child was.

'Who are you? What are you doing in this forest, dear child?' asked King Dushyant. The child did not reply and continued playing with the lion cub, opening its mouth to count its teeth. 'Who was this brave child? Who were his parents?' wondered the king.

A sound made him look up and there in the shadows of the trees, he saw Shakuntala, his beloved wife—the beautiful, gentle wife he had forgotten and abandoned.

Her eyes were sparkling with happiness as she smiled at him. 'This is our son, my lord. His name is Bharat,' she said.

King Dushyant could not stop the tears of joy streaming down his face as he picked up his son, who was handsome and brave. Shakuntala came and stood by him, as shy as a new bride. The gods had helped him to find her again and that is why the chariot had brought him to this remote part of the forest. 'Forgive me, my beloved, for forgetting you,' he whispered to her.

'It was not your fault, my king,' she said. Then she told him about the curse that had separated them for so many years. 'All of that is in the past. We shall be together now. It was our destiny to be parted and come together again. It has made our love stronger,' she said softly. Standing in a circle of love, they looked at their son. Somehow they knew their son Bharat would be a great king one day.

15

DAMYANTI & NALA

Trials and Tribulations in Love

'O Damayanti, noble princess!
Nala is present in your own heart
Then why do you pine for him?

O friend! He does, indeed, dwell in my heart,
It is his absence outside of me that torments me.

O Damayanti, the jewel of your being,
Split asunder by the fire of separation,
Your heart is bereft of ornaments.

O friend! If my lover is taken away from me
Then, even by the heart
I am done with.'

—Sriharsha, Naishadha Charita

The soothing, gentle sound of birdsong filled the air as Damayanti strolled in the palace garden at dawn. She plucked a freshly opened red champa blossom, still moist with dew, to adorn her hair, and when she lifted her face to look up at the sky, the clouds seemed to be dancing to a mysterious, joyous tune. Damayanti, the princess of Vidarbha, had everything a young woman could wish for—unmatched beauty, a noble lineage and a wealthy, doting family—yet she was often restless and sad. A strange ache filled her heart though she was surrounded by peace and tranquility.

'What is it that I long for? Who am I waiting for?' she asked herself, gazing at the clouds restlessly. Damayanti was famous all over the kingdom and in the lands beyond for her exquisite beauty. Many princes of the realm were eager to ask for her hand in marriage but Damayanti ignored them all. She had this unexplained feeling in her heart that someone was waiting for her; someone whom she would love with all her heart. 'I will wait. I know he will find me, if he truly loves me,' she said, consoling herself.

Far away, across emerald mountains and lakes, a king, handsome as a god, roamed in his palace gardens. Nala gazed up at the sky and tried to still his restive heart. 'What is this disquiet within me? Whom do I yearn for?' he said, his voice echoing in the vast garden.

Just then, he heard a musical trumpeting call and looked up. A flock of swans were flying over the palace garden and as Nala watched, one of them flew away from the flock and alighted near him. It was the most beautiful swan the king had ever seen. Its golden feathers shimmered in the sunlight and its eyes were like two rubies. Moving forward swiftly, Nala caught the swan with his hands, taking care not to hurt it. The bird trembled and then turned to him and spoke in a melodious, soft voice. 'O noble king. Release me. Spare my life.'

'I will not harm you, gentle creature. I will keep you in my garden and feed you the most delicious fruits,' said Nala.

'No. I must join my flock at once. Let me go and I will tell you about Damayanti, the most beautiful maiden on earth. I saw her strolling in the garden as we flew over her kingdom. It was dawn and the light was faint, yet her stunning beauty lit up the entire garden as if the moon had descended on earth by mistake. I flew down so close to you because I had to tell you that she is destined to be yours. I sensed the secret longing in your heart for her, even though you have never seen her.'

Nala was surprised and delighted to hear the words of the swan. He gently let go of the bird and stepped back but the swan did not fly away at once. It lifted its golden neck towards the king and spoke again. 'I shall be your messenger to Damayanti. I shall sing to her the very song that you hold deep in your heart and one day soon you shall be together,' said the swan as it flew away.

Nala stood for a long time looking up at the sky, his heart now brimming with joy. Though he had never seen her, he was madly in love with Damayanti already and longed to see her. 'Damayanti,' he whispered over and over again. 'Come to me, my love. You are my destiny, I know. Come to me soon or I shall die,' he said. From that day onwards, Nala roamed in the garden all day, waiting impatiently for a message. But the swan did not return. 'Has it forgotten about me? What should I do? How shall I find my love?' thought Nala, restless and anxious again.

The swan had not forgotten its promise to the king. The flock turned towards the south, flying over mountains and rivers, and finally they reached the kingdom of Vidarbha. The golden swan saw Damayanti on the balcony of the palace, gazing up at the sky, as if waiting for a messenger.

The swan flew down and alighted close to her and though Damayanti was startled, she did not move away. She sensed that something important was going to happen and waited, holding her breath.

'Hear my words, noble lady. The king of Nishadha is Nala, the most handsome man in the kingdom. He has heard of your beauty from me and now his heart is filled with longing for you, sweet princess. You reside in his breath and in his every thought. He loves you deeply and soon you will come to love him too. You have not seen each other, yet you both are meant for each other. This, I know, is the truth,' whispered the swan before it flew away.

Damayanti now surrendered herself to her unseen lover and felt a wave of happiness flood over her. Separated by mountains and rivers, by dense forests and lakes, the two lovers now felt they were somehow bound to each other by an invisible thread. They pined for each other, they longed to see each other and their hearts yearned to be together.

Damayanti had pledged her heart to Nala and thought about him day and night. Overwhelmed by this passion that had taken over her entire being, she began to grow weak and pale. 'When will I meet you, my beloved Nala?' she cried, staying awake all night, her lovesick heart in turmoil. She refused to talk to anyone and gazed at the sky all day, hoping for a message from her lover.

Her father and her brother soon noticed that something was wrong with the princess and began to get worried about her agitated state. 'She seems so restless, lonely and sad. Nothing seems to please her anymore. Maybe it is time to find her a husband. Let us arrange a grand swayamvar for her,' said her father.

'Yes. Damayanti is famed for her beauty. We will not lack suitors for her but we must choose the most valiant and noble prince from among them,' said her brother.

Soon, a grand swayamvar was organized and all the neighbouring kings and princes were invited to the ceremony. People talked of nothing else and Nala too came to hear about Damayanti's swayamvar. 'I must go to the kingdom of Vidarbha at once and make her my bride,' he said, and began to prepare for the long journey.

Then a strange thing happened. Just when Nala was about to start out from his palace, he met four unusual beings at the gate. They did not look like ordinary mortals and as soon as they began to speak, Nala knew they were gods.

He bowed to them, speechless with awe.

'O noble king. We are Indra, Agni, Varuna and Yama. We know you are on your way to Damayanti's swayamvar. We want to ask you to do something for us since we know you are always truthful, loyal and obliging,' they said. Indeed, Nala was known for his truthfulness.

Nala folded his hands and waited politely for them to continue.

'We want you to be our messenger and ask Damayanti to choose one of us as her husband,' they said in one voice.

Startled, Nala stared at the gods in dismay as a feeling of utter dejection swept over him. He could not refuse to do as they asked and yet how could he ask Damayanti to choose one of them when he himself had pledged his heart to her? There was nothing he could do now and Nala quietly touched the gods' feet and continued on his journey with a heavy heart.

With the powers that the four gods had bestowed on him, Nala entered the palace unseen and silently crept into Damayanti's chamber.

'Who are you? How have you entered my bedchamber? Are you human or a god?' she asked, surprised to see this handsome, tall man before her. She did not feel afraid of this stranger at all and a feeling of sheer happiness filled her entire being.

'I am Nala. I have come to you with a message from the gods Indra, Agni, Varuna and Yama. They want you to choose one of them as your husband tomorrow at your swayamvar,' said Nala, his voice broken with sorrow though his eyes were brimming with love. 'I am the one who loves you desperately; I am the one who wants to make you his wife,' his eyes were saying silently to her.

Damayanti looked at him and her happiness knew no bounds. She was surprised that he was giving her this message from the gods but she had her answer ready for him, 'My noble king. I have been waiting for you even since the golden swan told me about you. I already belong to you heart and soul and will wed no other man. I bow to the gods with respect but I will marry only you. Let them come to my swayamvar if they wish to, but I have already made up my mind to choose you. I, Damayanti, belong only to you,' she said, gazing at Nala, her beautiful face aglow with love.

Nala walked away, confused yet delighted. 'What shall I do now? I have to give her message to the gods. That is my duty but I know now she loves only me. Let us see what fate has in store for us,' he thought as he traced his steps back nervously to the waiting gods.

The gods were not pleased at all when they heard what Nala had to say and muttered angrily amongst themselves. 'We will proceed to the swayamvar and see what happens,' they said, giving Nala an ominous look.

All night long Nala stayed awake, gazing at the stars, his mind in turmoil. 'What if the gods take my beloved away? What if she changes her mind and choses one of them? After all, which woman would choose a human when she could marry a god?' he thought. Then Damayanti's beautiful face rose before his eyes and he heard her soft voice declaring her love for him. He smiled at the stars and said, 'No. She will never do such a thing. She promised me that she would choose me and only me. She knows we truly belong to each other.'

The next day at the swayamvar, the palace halls glittered as one by one the bejeweled and finely dressed kings and princes strode in and took their seats. They eyed each other nervously, each noble suitor wondering who would be the chosen one. Music played in the higher alcoves where the noble ladies sat and watched the proceedings. When Damayanti, dressed in the finest silken robes and adorned with jewels, walked in, a hushed silence fell over the gathering. Then, when she took her place at the dais, all those assembled gave a gasp of surprise. A beam of silvery light streaked down upon her head, lighting up her face and her beauty was enhanced a thousand times.

Damayanti looked around, her eyes searching for her beloved Nala, and then she gave a startled cry. There, right in front of her, were seated five handsome men and each one of them looked exactly like Nala.

Damayanti's heart began to race and she clutched the garland of flowers in her hand. 'What should I do now? The gods have decided to play a trick on me. How shall I find my prince Nala? How can I pick out my true love amongst them?' she said to herself. Then she shut her eyes and began to pray.

'O gods in heaven. Please help me. I have already chosen Nala as my husband and I have to be true to him. I pray to you to allow me to keep my sacred vow to be his wife. I seek your blessings, my gods. Please show me the real Nala so that I can place this garland upon him.'

The celestial beings heard her plea and their hearts melted. They knew she was truly devoted to Nala and they decided to help her. As Damayanti watched, the four gods rose gracefully and began to hover a few inches above the ground. Damayanti knew at once that only celestial beings could float above the ground and thus knew which one was the true Nala. Smiling quietly, she quickly stepped forward to the seated Nala and placed the garland around his neck. The heavens showered rose petals upon them as love emerged triumphant.

The assembled crowd began to cheer and even the disappointed kings and princes gave their blessings to Nala and Damayanti since they could see that they truly belonged to each other. They had never seen two people so in love with each other.

Damayanti's father, overjoyed to have Nala as a son-in-law, celebrated his daughter's wedding ceremony with great jubilation and organized a magnificent feast that carried on for days. Finally, after many days, the lovers were alone together and their wedded bliss knew no bounds. They gazed at each other with love and could not believe they were in each other's arms at last. From then on, Nala and Damayanti could not bear to be separated even for a moment. Their love for each other was so intense that it formed a magical bond between them. It was as if the entire universe had planned for them to be together forever. Anyone who beheld the lovers marveled at them and basked in the glory of their devotion to each other.

But far away, an evil eye glinted, watching the lovers with envy and malice. Kali, a malevolent spirit, had made up his mind to wed Damayanti ever since he had heard of her beauty. But when she had chosen Nala, he flew into a furious rage. 'How dare he take my chosen bride away from me? I will enter his body and I will slowly destroy him. Once he is ruined, Damayanti will abandon Nala and become mine,' he hissed and he prepared to steal into Nala's soul.

Years passed and Nala and Damayanti, unaware of what was going to happen, lived happily in the palace in total harmony and bliss. The gods showered them with more happiness and they were blessed with two children. Their kingdom flourished and they were adored, respected and admired by all.

All this while, the evil spirit Kali was waiting quietly in the shadows; waiting for the right moment to strike. He made many intricate and evil plans but could not achieve anything because of Nala's pious, noble nature. Finally, he came upon a devious plan. He changed himself into a human and befriended Nala's cousin Pushkara. This wicked cousin had always been very jealous of Nala and coveted his kingdom.

'I know how much you want to dethrone Nala and become the king. I will help you achieve your ambition. We will make Nala play a game of dice. That is his only weakness. I will make sure you win. Come, let us ruin him together,' whispered Kali in Pushkara's ears as he slept.

* * *

Damayanti felt a change in the sky and was surprised to see a streak of strange black shadows race across the sun. 'Is this a bad omen?' she wondered. But, totally content and happy with her life, she dismissed the thought.

At the same time, Pushkara approached his cousin Nala and invited him to play a game of dice. At first, Nala refused, but when Pushkara began to mock him, he reluctantly agreed. They sat down in a quiet corner of the palace and began to play. Kali crept into the dice and changed the course of the game. Then he stole into Nala and took over his soul. Over and over, Pushkara won and Nala lost. Though everyone around him tried to stop him from playing, Nala would not listen since the demon Kali now controlled his mind. Nala forgot about everything—his wife, his children, his kingdom—and all that mattered was the game of dice. The day changed to night as Nala and Damayanti's charmed life was ruined. Nala lost everything in the game—his palace, his wealth and his kingdom.

'Go away. Go live in the forest, brother. This kingdom is mine now. You are a pauper. You own nothing,' laughed Pushkara. Kali watched, his sinister eyes glowing in the shadows. He had finally ruined Nala; he had got his revenge.

Defeated, Nala left the palace at night and walked barefoot into the forest. 'I am so ashamed of what I have done. I don't know what got into my mind. Some evil spirit was forcing me to throw the dice over and over again even though I was losing. Now I must leave Damayanti, my beloved. The pain in my heart is unbearable,' he cried, as he stumbled down the dark paths of the forest. Then he turned around and saw Damayanti was following him.

'Wait for me. How did you think, my lord, that I would live all alone in my father's palace while you roamed the forests? You are my life and we will suffer this fate together,' she said.

'No, please take the children and go away to your father's kingdom. You will be safe there,' said Nala.

'I have sent the children to my father's kingdom but I will go with you. Do not think, even for a moment, that I shall leave your side,' said Damayanti. 'I cannot live without you. Your life is my life. We will get through this together, my love,' she said, tears running down her beautiful face.

Nala could not look into her eyes and bowed his head. Together, they started walking—Nala holding his wife's hand, moving the thorny shrubs out of her way. They roamed the forests for days, surviving on berries and nuts, their bare feet bleeding, their clothes torn. Damayanti tried her best to console her husband and begged him to go to her father for help. 'He will send an army to regain your kingdom,' she said. Nala refused to listen to her. A fragment of the evil spirit Kali still remained in his soul and Nala struggled with an inner battle to maintain his sanity. At night, weary and weak with hunger, the lovers held each other and wept quietly in the darkness. 'Will this torment ever end? Will we ever return to our old lives? How happy and content we were. How our love flourished like a thousand fragrant roses,' thought Damayanti, caressing her husband's rough, dusty hands. Wrapped in a single, torn garment, they stayed awake all night, seeking solace in each other's embrace.

After some time, Nala could no longer bear to see Damayanti wrecked by sorrow, fading away day by day, and he decided to leave her. His face distorted with anguish, his eyes blinded by tears, he silently walked away one night.

'Without me to hinder her she will find her way to her father's kingdom somehow and be safe there,' he thought, his mind confused as the demon Kali coiled and twisted inside him.

When Damayanti woke up at dawn, she reached her hand out and found an empty space next to her. She leapt up at once, trembling with fear. 'O, my lord, where are you?' she cried. When there was no answer, she fell down to the ground and began to sob. 'Why have you forsaken me? Where have you gone? How shall I live without you, my love? Please come back to me,' she wailed, hitting her head on the rocks till it bled.

Now all alone, dressed only in a torn garment, Damayanti wandered in the forest, crying her heart out. The creatures of the forest could not bear to see her grief and tried to console her in their own way. The birds sang near her while the trees showered her with blossoms but Damayanti did not see them. Her eyes blind with tears, she walked aimlessly, stumbling and falling as she went deeper and deeper into the dark forest, searching for her husband. 'Dearest, where are you?' she called over and over again, her voice growing weaker and feebler with each passing day.

After meandering for days she finally reached a big city. As she walked down the crowded street, people stared at her bedraggled, torn garment, her mud-streaked face and matted hair. 'Look at that mad beggar woman. Let's chase her away,' shouted the children of the city, throwing stones at her. Damayanti ran to seek shelter and ended up under the palace windows.

'Who is that?' asked the queen mother as she looked down at the woman cowering near the wall. 'She looks like a woman from a noble family even though her face is covered with mud and her garment is torn and dirty. Go fetch her to me,' she ordered her servants.

Weary and overwhelmed by despair, her heart full of pain, Damayanti sank down at the queen mother's feet.

'Who are you? Why are you in such a sorry state?' asked the queen mother in a kind voice.

'I am a most unfortunate woman who has lost her beloved husband. I have been roaming in the forest for days but I cannot find him. He lost his kingdom in a game of dice and we were living in the wilderness together but then we were torn apart by some evil force. I have lost my only love and I have no desire to live any more. Yet I must, for the sake of my two children,' said Damayanti, her voice broken with sorrow.

'Do not be so sad, my child. You must stay here in the palace with me. Consider this your home now. I shall send spies to comb each corner of the land and bring us news of your husband. Until then, rest here and regain your strength. You are like a daughter to me now,' said the queen mother, her eyes brimming with tears of compassion as she heard Damayanti's sad story. 'I will help you find your husband and one day soon you both will be united.'

Meanwhile, far away in the darkest depths of the forest, Nala was sitting by a rock, lamenting his fate. 'I have left Damayanti in this wilderness. What madness possessed me?' he cried, when suddenly the rock began to shake and then burst into flames. Nala looked up and found himself gazing into the eyes of a giant serpent. 'Save me, O king,' hissed the snake, twisting and turning in the fire, its form diminishing. Nala quickly reached forward and pulled the snake out of the blazing fire and placed it on a sheltered rock.

The snake uncoiled itself and said, 'I thank you for rescuing me from the fire. I was placed in the fire because of a curse and you have saved me. Now I will do you a favour. I know you have lost your kingdom and your queen but you will regain them both. Take ten steps forward.' Nala turned around and began to walk away but when he took the tenth step, the snake crept up and swiftly bit him. 'What have you done? I saved your life and this is how you thank me,' cried Nala. Then he looked down and saw that his body had changed and he was now a misshapen dwarf. Nala was shocked. 'What have you done to me, you ungrateful creature?'

The serpent spoke in a soft voice. 'Do not be alarmed, noble king. I have changed your form so that you can go about your tasks in disguise. Take this necklace of beads. When you wear them you will become your former self. Now adopt a new name and embrace the path ahead. Your beloved awaits you but first you must win your kingdom back,' said the serpent.

The snake disappeared and Nala made his way through the forest as swiftly as he could. The snake bite had sucked out Kali's poison from his soul and now his head was crystal clear and sharp again. 'I must find Damayanti. I have to find her as soon as possible,' he kept saying to himself.

Nala soon reached the kingdom of Ayodhya. There, concealed in his dwarf form, Nala became a charioteer to the king. He worked tirelessly in the stables, taking care of the king's horses. At night he would lie on the ground and gaze at the moon, thinking of his wife. Her beautiful face would loom in front of his eyes and he often heard her melodious voice calling his name. His heart would fill with longing and he would repeat her name over and over again. 'I hope and pray she has reached her father's kingdom. I will think of a plan and get to her somehow but first I must get my kingdom back,' he thought.

Meanwhile, Damayanti too thought about Nala day and night. At night she dreamt that they were walking in the forest together, arm in arm. Her heart filled with joy but then she would wake up and find herself alone. With sadness and an ache in her heart, she roamed the palace gardens, hoping she would catch a glimpse of the golden swan who had first told her about Nala.

'Where are you, my beloved? Why don't you come looking for me? You know I cannot live without you, yet why do you torment me so? My life is empty without you, noble husband. Come back to me,' she whispered to herself.

By now the queen mother had discovered Damayanti's identity and she and her children were safe in her father's kingdom. Damayanti's father, the king, was unhappy and sad to see his daughter's heartbroken, dismal state. He called a hundred messengers and sent them to faraway lands in search of Nala. But no one could find him since he was now a dwarf and not his former, handsome, godlike self. Then one day, Damayanti heard some news that gave her a glimmer of hope. 'I met a dwarf charioteer in the kingdom of Ayodhya. He is an expert with horses and also a great cook. He often talks about King Nala and how he was cheated out of his kingdom. He cried when he told me how the noble king lost his wife,' said the messenger.

'Could he be my beloved Nala? But this man is a dwarf. My husband is as handsome as a god,' thought Damayanti.

Then she thought of a plan. She went to her father and said, 'Father, please organize a swayamvar for me. I wish to get married again.'

Surprised and pleased, her father agreed at once. He wanted to see his daughter happy again. As the news of Damayanti's swayamvar spread, the king of Ayodhya heard about it too. He asked Nala to take him there. 'You are my best charioteer. You will get me there faster than anyone else. Go prepare to leave at once.'

Nala was heartbroken and shattered to hear that Damayanti wanted to marry again. 'She has given up all hope of ever meeting me again. I have waited too long to go to her. Yet, I feel in my innermost being that she is still true to me. Why is she then seeking another husband? Why has she agreed to this swayamvar?' he thought as he raced the chariot towards the kingdom of Vidarbha.

When Nala reached the palace in Vidarbha, his entire being stood still as he beheld Damayanti after so long. Her beautiful face was pale and her eyes were filled with sadness. She kept looking around as if searching for someone. The kings took their place, impatient for the ceremony to begin. Damayanti's eyes fell on Nala. 'I think it is he. But he has changed into a dwarf. How shall I find out if it is truly my Nala?' she thought. Damayanti looked at the dwarf again and he looked back at her and then quickly cast his eyes down. In that moment, Damayanti knew this dwarf was her husband. When he had looked at her, she had seen in his eyes the deep love that shone like a celestial light. She knew she was right. It was her Nala.

'I know who you are. You are my beloved husband. I have been searching for you ever since you left me in the forest that night. Please tell me that I am right,' said Damayanti to the dwarf, sobbing.

Nala lifted his eyes at last and nodded. He touched the beads around his neck and was transformed at once into his former self. The world stood still as Nala and Damayanti gazed at each other. They were united again at last.

However, Nala wanted to regain his kingdom first. 'Damayanti found me before I could do that. I want to bestow honour upon my queen. I cannot bear to be separated from her again but I will keep my pledge to get back my kingdom,'

Nala said as he walked in the forest, gazing up at the sky, hoping the Gods would help him.

Suddenly, a clever plan came into his head. After gathering a huge army of soldiers, elephants and horses and one white chariot he went to his former kingdom. He invited his evil cousin, who had cheated him earlier, to play a game of dice. 'I am no longer a novice at this game. While I was employed as a charioteer by King Rituparna he taught me all the secret tricks one can use in a game of dice and I have mastered every move. My cousin does not stand a chance against me now.'

At the first cast of dice, Nala defeated his cousin effortlessly and regained his kingdom once again. He forgave his cousin and allowed him to remain in the kingdom as he was a fair and benevolent ruler. Damayanti was happy to return to the palace once more and be with her beloved Nala day and night. 'Never will I part from you even for a moment, dearest,' he said to Damayanti, and the golden swans flying past called out joyous greetings to the lovers.

They blessed the couple as they left, saying, 'May your love blossom and grow forever like the blue lotus on a heavenly lake. May you be together forever.'

16

SARASWATI, LAXMI AND GANGA

Jealous Love

'At day's end
Fearing to lose her lover,
The Cakravaki bird,
One eye full of anger,
Watches the sun set.
[The] Other eye full of tears,
Watches her lover.
As a deceitful one,
Showing two feelings at once.'

—Chandraka

Vishnu, the Lord of Creation, was sitting peacefully on his resplendent throne in his golden palace at Vaikunth with his three wives. There was the sweet-tempered, gentle Laxmi, resplendent in gossamer red and bedecked with precious jewels; there was regal Saraswati, in pristine white silks, her beautiful face gleaming with intelligence and profound knowledge and the lively, turbulent Ganga, with her cascading, dark hair and sparkling eyes. All seemed calm and peaceful till Ganga, suddenly overcome with passion, sent a seductive glance at Lord Vishnu and he responded at once.

The sidelong, seductive glance she sent, as swift as a dart, was brimming with pure passion. As Ganga turned her face to look at her beloved Lord Vishnu, she felt her body tremble like a lotus blossom, unfurling in the wind. She longed to put her arms around him and pull him towards her. She needed his divine touch like a parched river needs the rain. She turned her head slightly and looked at him again, love pouring from her eyes, and this time she knew that the arrow of love she had sent, had reached him; she knew he felt the same overwhelming desire for her. Their eyes locked and an invisible thread of love and longing now pulled them towards each other. Ganga's heart flooded with delight. 'I want nothing more but to be with you eternally. Never let me live without you, my lord. Stay by my side forever and ever,' she said in her mind because she knew her Lord Vishnu could read her thoughts. It did not matter that they were not alone, her desire had reached him—she could tell by the gleam in his lotus eyes.

Ganga closed her eyes and remembered how she had emerged from Vishu's toe and was thus named Vishnupada. Their love was celebrated in the celestial world and she belonged only to him. Ganga knew that though he showed great affection to his other two wives Lakshmi and Saraswati, deep in his heart he hid a fiery passion only for her. 'My Lord Vishnu is mine alone,' she chanted in her mind, her heart filled with desire.

Ganga, lost in the tumultuous waves of love, did not notice that the golden pillars of Vaikuntha were suddenly struck by a beam of shimmering, white light and a strong gust of wind rushed in and began to swirl around the three seated goddesses. Dried, dusty leaves and stale flower petals dropped on their heads from nowhere. It was as if the heavens were predicting the turmoil that was about to erupt amidst them. Whispers of warnings ran through the golden palace but the three goddesses did not heed them.

Saraswati, lifted her finely chiseled beautiful face, now distorted with anger, to glare at Ganga. A furious rage swept over her entire body like wildfire and she felt the heat of anger rising in her heart like a serpent uncoiling. She tried to control herself but the fury would not subside. She had seen Ganga and her Lord Vishnu exchanging amorous, lustful glances and a jealous fury was now burning within her, filling her with bitter rage. She had never felt this kind of intense jealousy before for the other two wives of Lord Vishnu, but today Ganga had overstepped the mark. Ganga was trying to lure Lord Vishnu with her wanton behaviour, shamelessly making eyes at him in a most suggestive way right in front of them. 'Ganga, Laxmi and Saraswati. The lord loves us all but why is he showing such partiality to Ganga now? She is tempting him, she is trying so hard to entice him, and I cannot bear it,' thought Saraswati, as she narrowed her eyes and stared at Ganga sitting before her, smiling and simpering; so confident of being the lord's favourite wife .

Saraswati turned away as anger filled her body. 'Lord Vishnu and I share a pure, sublime love that no other God in the celestial world has ever seen or felt. I live on the tip of his tongue and his entire being belongs to me. We have been together for so many ages. He is my eternal lord. Ganga is nothing to him so why does he look at her in this way?'

As she watched Ganga, Saraswati's entire body began to quiver with anger and her fury now overflowed like molten lava. 'Look at her. How can she behave in this brazen manner? Does she not know that we are seated here too, in the presence of our lord? Has she forgotten that we are his wives too?' said Saraswati to Laxmi, who was sitting quietly next to her.

The serene Laxmi had noticed Ganga's amorous glances towards their lord but the placid, kindhearted goddess did not mind. Jealousy, envy or greed had never entered her pure heart. She knew she was Vishnu's true consort. As soon as she had emerged during the churning of the ocean, she had chosen him as her husband and they belonged to each other. The heavens had showered their blessings on their divine union. Whenever Vishnu incarnated to save the world, she always accompanied him. Ganga and Saraswati were her co-wives and she loved them too because her lord loved them.

The lovely goddess of benevolence rose quietly from her throne and stood near Saraswati. She touched Saraswati's hand gently. In a soft, sweet voice, she said, 'Let her be. Ganga is just being her playful self. She is always so turbulent and full of energy and her feeling of love often overwhelms her. We both know that our gracious and benevolent Lord Vishnu loves the three of us equally. Calm your jealous heart, sister. We live so amicably and peacefully at Vaikuntha with our lord. Please do not let your jealous anger destroy our glorious, heavenly life.'

Saraswati pushed her away and Laxmi almost stumbled and fell against a pillar. Saraswati did not bother to help steady her. Instead she tossed her head haughtily and cried, 'How can you sit so placidly while they enact this love play right before us? It is as if we have become invisible to them. Look at Ganga's face. It is flushed not just with pleasure but pride too. She thinks that our Lord Vishnu loves her more than he loves us. I fear that she might just steal him away from us forever. She is a terrible, wicked creature with a greedy heart.' Tears of rage welled up in Saraswati's eyes.

'Hush. Lord Vishnu and Ganga will hear your harsh, hurtful words. I think we should leave them alone. Come. Let us go and sit in the garden. The cool, scented breeze from the heavenly blossoms will calm your jealous rage,' said Laxmi, moving slowly and reaching her hand out to take Saraswati's hand in hers.

'No. No. Leave me alone. How can you be so naïve and unsuspecting? Can't you see that Ganga wants us to go away forever? Then she can be the only wife to Lord Vishnu. I will not take a single step away from here. Let her hear what I have to say. She deserves my cruel words. Let our lord, too, hear what I have to say. I am not afraid to speak the truth. I am not a coward like you. You go sit in the garden, if you want. You are a timid, docile and foolish creature. I hate you for taking Ganga's side. You have betrayed me by doing this,' shouted Saraswati, and the entire palace heard her angry words and shook their heads in dismay. They had never seen such a quarrel take place in heavenly, tranquil Vaikuntha.

'How will Lord Vishnu cope with this terrible strife amongst his wives? What will he do now?' the gods asked each other. Some were amused by this strife while others worried about the outcome of this bitter quarrel between the three great goddesses.

Lord Vishnu heard Saraswati's angry tirade and lifted his hand in a benevolent gesture. 'Calm down, beloved wife. You three are my most precious wives; my precious jewels. Each one of you lives in my heart. I love each one of you equally. I am not partial to any single one amongst you,' he said with a gentle smile.

But Saraswati's jealous heart, now raving with a stormy, uncontrollable passion, would not quieten down and she began to speak angrily to her husband.

'How can you say that you love us equally when you spend so much time with Ganga? She is always clinging to you while Laxmi and I sit far away from you—as this is deemed proper for your consorts. Everyone in Vaikuntha can see this unfair, partial behaviour of yours, my lord, yet you declare that you love all three of us equally. You never reprimand Ganga for her wanton behaviour. You indulge her every little whim,' said Saraswati, her voice, always melodious and sweet, now harsh and broken with bitterness and anger.

'Listen to me, Saraswati. You are harming yourself by letting this jealous rage overwhelm you. Look at Laxmi. How peaceful and calm she is. She never gives Ganga those angry looks like you do all the time. You must learn to control your excitable temper and your bitter, hate-filled speech. I love you all equally, I have said it so many times. Yet you do not believe me, my lovely wife,' said Lord Vishnu calmly.

'You say these meaningless words just to keep us quiet. Laxmi might believe you but I do not. I am not a fool. O, Hari, you are partial to Ganga and I can feel it in my heart. You long to be with her all the time. I can tell by looking at the amorous gazes that flow between you two constantly like a river of passion. Even in our presence, your eyes search for her all the time. You don't know how much pain this causes me. Laxmi does not seem to mind since that is her nature but I cannot share you with Ganga anymore. I feel so deprived of your love. My life is not worth living. You are a cruel one, my lord, to treat me like this. I might as well as give up my life here and now,' she said and began to sob.

Lord Vishnu could no longer tolerate her angry tirade and walked away.

Saraswati watched him leave, seething with rage, and then turned to Ganga. 'See what you have done. You, shameless one. Our lord has left our presence because of you. Why did you cast those seductive looks at him? You think you own him. You think he loves you the most amongst us three. I will show you that you are worth nothing to him. I will destroy you,' said Saraswati, pointing an accusing finger at Ganga.

Laxmi, embarrassed and upset by Saraswati's deranged behaviour, went to calm her down but Saraswati's anger had taken over her entire being and now she turned her fury towards Laxmi. 'Go away and leave me alone. You are always taking Ganga's side. I don't want to see you or talk to you,' she said, pushing Laxmi away and advancing towards Ganga, waving her arms frantically and trying to threaten her. Laxmi rushed forward and stood between the two. This incensed Saraswati even more. 'Why are you trying to protect her? Why do you care for her so much? Can you not see she is stealing our lord from us? Are you blind? Move out of the way,' shouted Saraswati, putting both her hands on Laxmi to push her away. Laxi stood by her side and tried again and again to placate Saraswati by whispering soothing words to her but the goddess of speech would not listen.

Suddenly, she lifted her hand and pointed to Laxmi. 'I hate you for taking Ganga's side. I curse you now. You will become a plant and go and live on earth,' she screamed.

Ganga now rushed towards Saraswati. 'What have you done? Gentle Laxmi has done you no harm. Why did you curse her? Have you lost your mind?' she shouted, trying to protect Laxmi with her body.

Saraswati looked at Ganga with such hatred and fury in her eyes, that Ganga stepped back at once. She was now afraid of what the goddess, deranged with anger, would do. Fear clutched her heart as she heard Saraswati's next words.

'I curse you too,' she said, lifting a trembling finger. 'I curse you, thief of my husband's heart. May you become a river and flow amongst mortal men on earth. They will wash their sins in your waters forever and ever. You have no place in heaven now with my Lord Vishnu. Go away and never let us see you again in Vaikuntha,' screamed Saraswati, her beautiful face contorted with anger.

'Stop behaving like a mad creature. See how angry you have made our Lord Vishnu. He has gone away from us. Sit quietly now and think of what you are saying. Take back your curse on innocent Laxmi,' said Ganga.

'I will not do any such thing, you wretched, shameless creature. I curse both of you again and again. Remember that the power of my words surpasses everything in this world. Know that you are cursed and cursed by me forever,' shouted Saraswati.

Ganga stood very still and then she spoke in a quiet, cold voice. 'I curse you, Saraswati, to become a river on earth. Like us, you too shall no longer live with our Lord Vishnu; like us, you will also suffer a lonely life on earth.'

A storm now began to rage through the heavenly palace, creating a turbulent, discordant atmosphere. The perpetual serene golden light of the palace faded as if darkness had fallen, though it was the middle of the day. All the other heavenly creatures looked around in dismay. They did not know what had happened and began questioning each other, running around in confusion. The heavenly birds stopped singing and the moon and the stars sped away to hide. Magnificent Vaikuntha, the seat of Lord Vishnu, became a desolate, silent abode.

When Vishnu returned and learnt what had happened, he was shocked and distraught. 'What have you done to each other? How did this frenzy of jealousy swallow you three? O Saraswati, why did you invoke your powerful curses on Ganga and Laxmi? Why did you send them down to earth?

What madness overtook you? You too have been cursed by Ganga to become a river on earth! How shall I get you three back to heaven?' he said, pacing up and down, twisting his hands in despair.

He knew he could not erase Saraswati's powerful curses upon Ganga and Laxmi. 'I cannot believe that my Laxmi, my placid, gentle Laxmi will go away from me due to no fault of hers,' he said.

He wondered how he could redeem these terrible curses. He wanted Ganga and Laxmi to be by his side but he no longer wanted Saraswati. Her fierce temper was now making her impossible to live with. He turned to face his wives.

'This is what I will do. Ganga, you will flow down on earth from Shiva's locks but one part of you shall remain in heaven with me. Laxmi, you will become the river Padma and also the sacred tulsi plant, but wherever you grow on earth, I shall be not far from you as the sacred shaligram stone. You, my heart, my gentle one, will be worshipped by all the people on earth in your tulsi form. One day you shall return to me and we will be together again forever,' he said.

Holding back her unshed tears, Laxmi glanced at Lord Vishnu. She suddenly caught a glimmer of a strange, mysterious light in his eyes. 'Did he know this was going to happen?' she wondered, her heart heavy with the thought of leaving Vaikuntha and her lord. She tried very hard to console herself with the thought that he would always be by her side, but the tears continued to fall. With loving, gentle tenderness, Lord Vishnu picked her up in his arms and wiped the tears from her face. 'We shall be close to each other even on earth. Remember, where you grow as the auspicious tulsi plant, I will be right by your side as the shaligram. You will always feel my presence,' he whispered.

Vishnu's next words were for Saraswati, who now stood silently by a pillar, stunned by what she had done. Remorse and regret churned in her heart and confused thoughts raced in her head. What madness had possessed her? Why had she behaved in this way? Would her lord ever forgive her? Her jealousy, hatred and rage slowly dissolved as Vishnu spoke to her in a calm voice.

'Go live on earth as a river. Think of all that has passed and allow yourself to be kind and forgiving. Reflect on your fiery temper and your thoughtless words of anger and then when you calm down, you shall become a sacred, cleansing river and people on earth will worship you for hundreds of years. After a few ages have passed, you shall come back and live as Brahma's wife in heaven. I shall still retain a small part of you. Go peacefully and let love towards mankind heal your burning, jealous rage forever,' said Lord Vishnu. He then retreated into a quiet corner to regain his peace of mind. The air around him grew fragrant once more as the heavenly white and blue lotus blossoms began to bloom one by one in Vaikuntha.

The soothing words spoken by their beloved lord soon turned into music as the three goddesses swept down to earth. Ganga twisted and turned in Shiva's locks for a while before flowing on earth as the river. Tulsi quietly began to grow in sacred groves and people soon realized her healing powers and began worshipping her along with the sacred stone, the shaligram. Saraswati flowed on earth for countless centuries and whoever sat along her banks gained deep knowledge. Wherever they appeared on earth, the three goddesses heard his celestial song in their hearts, and they knew Lord Vishnu would be with them for an eternity.

ACKNOWLEDGEMENTS

I would like to thank Ranjana Sengupta of A Suitable Agency and my editor Ridhima Kumar at HarperCollins India for their excellent editorial inputs and many lively conversations about love, romance and heartbreaks—in heaven and on earth.

ABOUT THE AUTHOR

Bulbul Sharma is an author and artist. Her works are in the collection of the National Gallery of Modern Art, Lalit Kala Akademi and Chandigarh Museum as well as in private collections in India and abroad. She has published several books including *My Sainted Aunts, The Perfect Woman, Anger of Aubergines, Banana Flower Dreams, ShayaTales, Devi, Eating Women, Telling Tales, Now That I Am Fifty, Tailor of Giripul, Grey Hornbills at Dusk, Murder at the Happy Home for the Aged* and *Love and Learning Under the Magnolia*. Her books have been translated into Italian, French, German, Chinese, Spanish and Finnish. Her books for children are *Fabled Book of Gods and Demons, The Children's Ramayana, Walking Through the Hills* and *Secret Tales from the Himalayas*. She conducts painting and storytelling workshops for special needs children and is a founding member of Sannidhi, an NGO that works in the village schools of Himachal Pradesh.

ABOUT THE AUTHOR

[illegible]

HarperCollins *Publishers* India

At HarperCollins India, we believe in telling the best stories and finding the widest readership for our books in every format possible. We started publishing in 1992; a great deal has changed since then, but what has remained constant is the passion with which our authors write their books, the love with which readers receive them, and the sheer joy and excitement that we as publishers feel in being a part of the publishing process.

Over the years, we've had the pleasure of publishing some of the finest writing from the subcontinent and around the world, including several award-winning titles and some of the biggest bestsellers in India's publishing history. But nothing has meant more to us than the fact that millions of people have read the books we published, and that somewhere, a book of ours might have made a difference.

As we look to the future, we go back to that one word—a word which has been a driving force for us all these years.

Read.

Harper Collins

Harper Sport

HARPER FICTION

HARPER NON-FICTION

हार्पर हिन्दी

HARPER LEARNING

HARPER VANTAGE

HCCB HARPERCOLLINS CHILDREN'S BOOKS

4th

HARPER PERENNIAL

HARPER DESIGN

BOOKTOPUS

HARPER BUSINESS